THE SCI-FI TALES COLLECTION

Gary Alexander Azerier

ISBN: 978-93-6354-406-2

Second Edition: 2025
Rs. 200/-

Cyberwit.net
HIG 45 Kaushambi Kunj, Kalindipuram
Allahabad - 211011 (U.P.) India
http://www.cyberwit.net
Tel: +(91) 9415091004 +(91) (532) 2552257
E-mail: info@cyberwit.net

Printed at Repro India Limited.

THE Sci-Fi Tales Collection
by Gary Alexander Azerier

SPACE STUFF

TIME STUFF

INFINITE PROBABILITY

DREAMS

DIMENSIONS

INTRODUCTION

Science-Fiction stories comprise tales which contemporary science would deem beyond possibility. The stories speculate "what if".... What if a fleet of spaceships looking for a new world break loose of its home galaxy and attain unheard of speeds beyond the cosmic limits? What happens to a man's mind when a lone astronaut finds himself stranded on a farthest imaginable alien planet? What adventure awaits a young boy who can access a train which travels to stellar constellations? But science-fiction travels beyond space. It can present a situation in which a grown man returns to his childhood home, long gone, and visits himself - as a child. It can look in on time travelers who miscalculate their journeys and find themselves on different and irreconcilable time coordinates...presenting themselves with insurmountable options.

Science-Fiction can resurrect ghosts confronting a man with a shade, a phantom, who strangely appears and vanishes in an old, recently purchased photo. It can reawaken dreams and reunite spirits from across spans of time and space, and can create a fourth dimension from oddly shaped blocks and a glass bauble. In the turning of a page it can disclose what happens when a madman attempts to discover ancient reflections trapped in a mirror, and can show us what may befall cities of the future; what terrors await.

Science-Fiction can render the improbable, probable but can also reach hopes and dreams that lay beyond...hidden in the folds of reason, in change, in space and time.

Science-Fiction may not offer precepts, tenets, morals and code for which to strive and those by which to live...but it can offer dream and fantasy...the impossible...and that which science has n achieved...yet!

GAA

(ALMOST TWO BAKER'S DOZEN...)

Infinite Probability....Pasts & Futures...Dreams & Dimensions
Fantasy & Reality....Time and Travel....Space & Speed
Wraiths, Shades, Phantoms and Ghosts
Stars

AD ASTRA!

SPACE STUFF

ORBITS

Much ado has been made, speculated, and even assumed recently, over the unseen, unheard, unfelt and untasted presence of what is appropriately termed "dark matter". Whatever it is...*if* it *is* at all, does not *reflect* light (nor does it interact with light in any way) placing investigators with one major disadvantage, as additional probative characteristics of "dark" matter remain hidden or, perhaps, more correctly, unexplained, as its inexplicable effects confound physicists, astronomers, cosmologists and philosophers, abandoning them in...the dark.

What prompts attention to this elusive actor is the mystery behind the characteristic shapes and sizes of the more than 200 billion observable galaxies...stretched billions of light years across space-time. It is the invisibility and the power, keeping their (?) components, planets, stars and myriad elements in the majestic and regal order which begs *some* explanation identifying *some* causative force, though none is apparent. The search is for the generator as well as the supporter of what uniformly binds <u>and</u> maintains the seemingly endless grand galactic elegance together.

An insignificant bit of catalyst might be overlooked, carelessly or intentionally, but despite the overwhelming physical mass throughout the apparent endlessness of space (and what we would tend to infer from our senses...through Hubble and Webb) dark matter, along with its equally strange and invisible partner, dark energy, leave the matter that we *do* see to figure a mere five percent of the equation at best, with the "dark" duo claiming more than 95 percent of the universe's mass albeit without any tangible, physical cause! Consequently, the nature of whatever comprises this stuff, and the solution to the questions it poses, becomes more...weighty!

Considering its invisibility, the force exerted by the dark duo is not electromagnetic nor does it appear to conform to what Albert Einstein proposed as the generator, the effectuator, of gravity, that is deep curves, bends and valleys in the very fabric of space. What little evidence stubbornly remains, however, when cancellations vaporize other possible candidates in the investigation, is, however weakly, gravity. But where is its origin? How does it operate?

Newton's law of gravity states that all objects assert a force upon one another...that all objects attract one another (inversely as the square of the distance between them). But Newton was unable to assign the *cause* of gravitational power. He could not identify the motion that produced the force of gravity! For Einstein, the essence of the gravitational force is not mass, but energy and warped space-time. And now, there recently have even been new challenges to both Newtonian and Einstein theories of gravity, as acceleration deviations have appeared between binary stars.

Indeed, it is a mix, as segments of theories and observations overlap and new ideas come to bear. It is in the face of this jumble and pursuit of perhaps a key piece of the inexorable puzzle that the following is presented:

Consider: an electron orbiting an atomic nucleus somewhere in space. Around and around it goes at let us say incalculable speeds. Now take that package, electron and nucleus, orbiting, as it most assuredly does, the moon...as the moon, some 250,000 miles away, similarly orbits the earth, at some 2,250 miles per hour.

Oddly, but well understood, and necessarily so, the earth, some 93 million miles from the sun, orbits our star, at some 67,000 miles per hour, just as the sun (of which some may be unaware) is on *its* way, from its arm at the outer edge of our Milky Way Galaxy...on *its* orbit, at approximately 500 thousand miles per hour...around the galaxy of some 200 thousand light years; a journey which will take our star approximately

225 million earth years to complete. But the fractal-like odyssey is not over, as we near our strange proposition.

Although the Milky Way is currently on a collision course with Andromeda there is speculation this may not occur. (We have some five billion years to find out). And if it will not, our galaxy will most likely resume *its* orbital course around the Virgo cluster, 50 million light years away, which may, in turn, eventually be headed for *her* neighbor, the Virgo Super cluster, a mere 67 million light years away.

The occasion of these meetings, however, is in doubt, as the *expanding* universe seems to be precluding these encounters as the root attractive force. Perhaps it *was* the mysterious attraction which had drawn independent bodies, through step by step sets of orbits, via its unseen dimensions, although now, it may be the expanding universe itself, skipping its final steps, to reveal itself prematurely. The final pull of our neighbor, a white star universe replete with its overwhelming mass of infinite density and energy has managed to pull and expand its entire sister. A blunder, whose author, despite so finely an orchestrated plan, over millennia, has rushed the final orbital steps. It suddenly appears as if the *entire universe* is going. Changes; Life full of surprises; best laid plans! We can only wait and see.

All of us are merely here to speculate, observe and report. In the end, after all, the performance is only smoke, mirrors, and... orbits. Round and round.

On his 104th birthday, I asked an old friend where he had been. “I’m here,” he replied. “I’m not going anywhere....”

THE LAST STAND

On the corner of 178th Street and Fort Washington Avenue, diagonally across the street from the old YMWHA, on whose site is now the Port Authority Bus Terminal, there was a wooden, olive drab newsstand. In the evening you could pick up a late paper or perhaps a copy of The Saturday Evening Post before hopping aboard the downtown number four, fifth avenue bus. The newsy who carried just about everything inside the little hovel was a one armed World War I vet who rarely spoke, but who knew all his customers, as they knew him, and who warmed the night corner with the flickering yellow light that glowed inside his booth. He sat quietly, some nights in a thirties newsy's cap, sometimes in his wool seaman's cap and ragged pea coat, as he awaited his last few customers for the late edition papers. In his heart he had long tired of the same faces, people coming and going, while he sat and watched, and waited, and dreamed. It seemed as if he had long tired of the repeated amenities; the token exchanges. He never smiled.

Well beyond the visor of the frayed tweed cap he wore on this night, the old eyes in his craggy face turned toward the black sky and the stars afar, deep into so many nights. He might have created alien craft soaring out from the heavens, settling some distance before his Earthly establishment to dispatch a dashing, or otherwise, spaceman toward him. And as the chilly winds blew along the George Washington Bridge from the rolling Hudson beneath it, certainly, he may have mused, the stranger and his companions, if there were any, should be drawn by his light, and should like to read of all the Earthly news. To the spaceman he would casually say, unruffled: "Paper, mister?"

But there was no ship. No spaceman; frequently no customers at all at this hour. Not yet.

***

He had journeyed, or so the records indicated, through the black vastness, the deep and empty reaches of space. Such a void of depth and emptiness did he traverse, that he had only to sleep through it; a sleep as deep, empty and black as those forever night realms through which he passed unknowingly. The hulking, silvery ship had carried him millions upon millions of miles through bleak and blurry light years from home to….

Now the rays of a warm sun, a different sun, beat down on the ship's multi-layered windows as the polyplex alloy shades lifted, filling the hulk's inner chambers with real light. And as his waking moments took shape in the swaddling of his cryochamber it seemed like a fresh Saturday morning. But it was not.

He had last been awake some months earlier. It was a Thursday, then. It seemed like only hours ago, but checking the readout on the ship's computer, the M330, he found it to be sixteen weeks.

He rose, washed, exercised and dressed. Then he ate. Checking further readouts on the M330 he flicked from line to bar graph, from color spectrum to texture, temperature and density scans. All the sequences were congruent. It was somewhat of a comfort. All seemed to be as expected.

Winston and Effington might have been pleased that, so far, all was going according to program. He felt the vacuum of their absence; the fear of being alone, but he had already dealt with the nightmare of his crewmembers' early and untimely demise months…years ago, when the accident occurred. He accessed their factor input charts and watched the printout of the substitution program he had affected with mission control when they were still reachable. The variables of Winston and Effington had been modified accordingly and the necessary accommodation made. CONTROL had wiped the slate and rewritten the mission in mid-flight. Winston and Effington had never existed. But, he thought as he peered out the gaping polyplex window into the pulsing dark violet glow of the new sun, they had.

For four days and four nights in the new time, he orbited the pink sun's world making preparations for the ship's touchdown. He worked, watched and dreamed as he shouldered his triple load. He pondered the ship, himself, the mission and what awaited below.

The vessel had been through all of it. He had not. But, he thought with some guilt, he had survived. There was a certain pride in that. Now, however, the success of the mission's completion, and it was a considerable task, would be up to him...alone. He had a momentary heady sensation as he contemplated the changeover from automatic pilot to manual shifting. There was no one else to fall back on.

The constant and unbroken cloud cover, whose chemical composition was still in the process of being analyzed by M330, was growing into a source of depression. It gnawed at the thin shell of patience which still managed to contain his curiosity. From time to time M330 showed enough latitude in conditions for him to drop altitude, which he did, but to little avail. The upper reaches of this stratosphere, with its heavy haze, seemed boundless despite the computer's indications to the contrary. The ship nonetheless continued its easy spiral descent, quietly, until he noticed the change in the darkening purple pulsing outside.

He was not sure as to its cause, but M330 revealed the answer on its summary screen. First, each of its line and bar readouts showed a glitch where one should not have been. The aberration was apparent alongside its twin comparison trip program model. With each subsequent readout revealed by the wipe, the irregularity widened. Then the computer began showing variants of the glitch elsewhere along the lines and bars. These seemed to correspond to the pulsing outside.

On one of M330's sub screens a trouble-shooting program operated on a one-step ahead, factor-isolation principle. On it, a color depiction of the planet's rising sun loomed impressively. At its near quadrant on the face of the star there was a tiny fleck. He might have overlooked the spot had it not been blinking like a cursor. He considered manually expediting the ship's spiral descent when the unexpected impact occurred. It jarred him, but was more like an electro-static charge going through the entire ship. When he regained his senses and stood up to the relief and realization that he was still alive, he noticed that ensuing readouts on M330 failed to make complete sense. One, however, did. One of the ship's reverse thrusters was knocked askew by the shock, and without them a safe touchdown would not be possible. He saw too, one of the stabilizing gyros was thrown off and the ship was now losing altitude at an alarming rate. Further, there appeared to be a terrible turbulence outside. If he could realign the thrusters and at least modify the gyro problem he might have a chance. But it would take time; at least an Earth hour or two. Fortunately the atmosphere of the huge planet below was that deep: a minimum, according to M330's charts, of three to four thousand miles from where he might be now.

With no little difficulty, jostled and bounced, he worked his way aft to reach what needed getting at. At one point, between adjustments which ended in the ship's listing, he noticed her cutting through the haze of strange clouds. The magenta pulsing was gone. The blackness was becoming sharp and clear. There was nothing visible out there now; not even a blurry fog by which he could gauge his movement. It looked as if he were not moving at all. But miles below, he knew, off to his right, was a white ball; quiet and slightly phosphorescent.

Outside the ship was a stillness that enveloped her; permeated her. He had arrived, coming in. He wondered to what. As the time passed the ball grew larger; its phosphorescence diminishing; another layer of cloud-cover becoming apparent. He thought his silver ship gliding in over the planet must look majestic, impressive, but wondered: to whom? There were moments of expectation. There were flashes of...something more than just haze, night and barren landscape, but they were only flashes, no more than that.

Combining as much precision with haste as he possibly could, he replaced one of the damaged thruster's parts and the affected gyro was realigned. M330, however, was responding only partially, half-wittedly. He had no time to delve into its circuitry. But he ran a final readout, all of which seemed plausible, and assumed the controls. It was the last stage of the descent with touchdown quickly approaching.

His orbit had just eased him around to the night side of the planet and the big star was setting rapidly. This was not on the program. Margin of error was not half the planet. But it was too late for a correction. He was too low and his spiraling approach and rate of descent could not accommodate it. The thrusters were activated and he felt the ship list. Suddenly there was a wave of nausea and as it continued it was punctuated by periodic perspiration. He had the thought that the prospect of death, no matter where in the universe one happened to be, carried with it the same terrifying anguish. Then he began to ponder, once again, Control's mission.

A relatively nearby galaxy and each of several solar systems within it were selected on the basis of proximity, accessibility and promise. That is to say, was there at least a probability the mission might bear fruit? The planet below him now was not known to bear life, but could sustain life. M330 and crew would reach it, explore it, mark it, seed it, and if possible retrieve at least one of the long dormant satellites and probes we dispatched. The usual quota of soil, rock, vegetation and liquid samples would be expropriated; experiments conducted on site; logs kept; transmitters erected; cameras set in place; monuments raised and a systematic search for life conducted.

But now, somehow, the mission seemed absurd to contemplate seriously. Survival and the question of what follows that were higher on his priority list of considerations. There would be plenty of time to execute Control's laundry list once he safely set foot down on…whatever it was down there.

Down there. It was a good deal closer now. It had, in fact, as its terrain filled M330's entire major viewing screen, by its growing proximity, transformed itself into reality. Soon, if he lived, he would be enmeshed in that reality, confident that it would be a reality not altogether dichotomous with his own. It would simply be an extension of his own reality. And yet, staring into the holographic viewing screen, it occurred to him that what he saw and was about to encounter was not so strikingly alien to him and could have existed anywhere. And this was, in fact, anywhere. It was just about as far "anywhere" as anyone so far as he knew had ever gone. For moments he attempted to grasp, in his terms, just how far. He did not dwell on it. It was relative, wasn't it? The illusion, if not the reality, remained: It did not seem far. It could be…home.

The thruster had been firing for some time. A warning sound and the unmistakable voice of ailing M330 directed him to strap in and prepare for the final phase of braking and the last series of spirals before touchdown.

It was night. Purple night and he seemed to be gliding deeper into it as occasional patches of light came to him and faded. Still it remained clear. For interminable stretches the terrain was unchanged, and unwavering night was bathed in unspoiled clarity. He maneuvered, corrected and remaneuvered. Then, unexpectedly, the ship slowed on its own and helplessly banked as it had hours before in the pulsing. As if in a Herculean attempt to correct itself it shocked the heavy stillness with an ear splitting report, sounding as if her giant hull had cracked. She did not right herself, jolted, and then slammed into the planet's brush and soil, askew.

When at last he was able to pry open the hatch of his dying ship he paused to marvel that he was alive. Then, he looked deeply, reflectively and with awe into what surrounded him. The hulking ship had somehow fallen onto an elevated embankment from which he thought he could make out yards of relatively flat terrain, long clumps and stretches of brush and more flatland. Far off to his left low cliffs formed a valley with this land on which he now stood, and configured a jagged outline of what seemed like ebony totems against the foreign sky. The steep and forbidding walls draped the scene menacingly but the fresh air was so still and the pitch so quiet as not to presage anything, good or evil.

He waited for morning but it did not come. Perhaps he had slept through it. He couldn't be sure as M330 was no longer providing reliable indications of anything. Going through the ship he laid out the standard lines of equipment which would enable the first of several excursions he was planning. At least his rover cart was working.

Not planning a lengthy exploration at first, he packed the buggy with a few essentials, lowered it from the ship and stood beside it, once again surveying this undisturbed indigo whose domain he was about to invade. It was then he saw it. He blinked his eyes. Far down into the valley, and then up, atop one of the flanking slopes there was a flicker, steady and distinct, like a beacon. It was the singular feature at the apparent terminus of the long landscape to draw and captivate his attention. He got into the RC1 and headed toward the light.

Most of the light that served to illuminate the terrain before him came from several moderately sized moons. Together, though, they did not reflect as much light as Earth's one satellite; nor did there seem to be as many stars overhead as on a clear Earth night.

The RC1 buggy bounced and jiggled but tugged its load without too much strain. At times it seemed to glide through hardly any ground resistance as it dashed toward the light. But the glowing light did not change in size or brightness. It did not appear to be getting any closer.

It was more than a night's ride, he wanted to rest but he would not allow himself to and he would not turn back. It was still black night and the valley was endless. From time to time long patches of thicket would fall between his line of sight and the beacon, but always, as the buggy sped through to the clearing that lay ahead, the yellowish flicker reappeared, undisturbed.

Occasionally he dozed momentarily consumed with fatigue, only to be jarred awake by a bounce, snapped into a quick consciousness parallel with a panicky scan of the horizon. He knew he had slept, not so much by his abrupt awakenings but, by the dream imagery his mind had begun to form during these mini naps. At first, no more than converging lines and quilty patches formed his images, but as his exhaustion increased the lines took on more intricate shapes and the patches dissolved into speedy, senseless mini-plots. One such plot saw several suns rising at various points along the planet's horizons creating an enormous convergence of shadow which, when combined with the sunlight, blocked out both the beacon and its site…and it was lost to him.

Another dream had him traveling away from an ever receding light source only to discover it being a faint star on the horizon. The dreams continued until the dark, flanking slopes gradually leveled out and, to his astonishment, he found himself on an equal plane with the amber twinkle. It was only then he rested and had something to eat.

The RC1 had plenty of muon fuel and seemed in fine shape. Still, there was a substantial area of thicket ahead, and while taking a short exploratory on foot, mostly for exercise, he opted to go the distance that way now that he could clearly make out the glimmer through the bramble. And perhaps walking might change his luck.

He was quite unaware of the passage of time, more so of distance. Only once, and only for an instant, did he give thought to the ship, envisioning it much farther down the plain than it was in actuality. But with ship and cart behind, quite alone now, he began to stumble.

The beacon was now beginning to come into focus through the brush, as the low star grouping on the horizon, of which his yellow gleam might have been a member, became obscured. He ran through the tangle of thorny vegetation that cut and pierced his suit and scratched his steamy visor until he removed it. A solitary figure in this alien planet night, he stumbled and pulled himself forward, tearing through the undergrowth of this remote sphere, this forlorn point in nowhere, everywhere, anywhere.

The dark green wood thinned and parted and cast out its visitor. It was almost within reach, he thought, as he looked up. And then some three hundred yards down, for the first time, he thought he could see it clearly. It stood alone: a beat up, painted over, olive drab, wooden, dimly lit newsstand. Inside, under a slightly flickering yellow light, half hidden behind a stack of freshly printed newspapers was a wizened, tweed-capped, newsy. From beneath a backdrop of sweets and crisply colored magazines, the newsy, no smile on his craggy face, drew out a late paper. The hardly discernable breeze that it fanned forth bore the scent of ink. The old man held it out. “Paper, mister?” he said.

He groped for change in his suit, bought one of each late edition, a couple of pulp magazines, Collier’s and the Saturday Evening Post. He bought peanuts, Life Savers and a plain Hershey Bar.

He would go back to the ship now, catch up on all the news, read the funnies, do the puzzles, maybe even listen to the radio. Why not? It was Saturday night! So what if he was alone? He was alone before.

***

Four point four light years away, on planet Earth, a craggy faced newsy in a tweed cap, tucked inside his newsstand and the lonely night on Fort Washington Avenue, under a flickering yellow light, awaited his last few customers for the remaining late edition papers. But in his heart he had long tired of the same faces, the familiar amenities, the well worn exchanges. Beyond the visor of his cap his tired eyes turned toward the night sky and the stars and galaxies afar, deep within it. His vision created alien craft soaring out from the heavens, settling before his Earthly establishment and dispatching a dashing spaceman toward him. Certainly, he mused, the stranger and his companions aboard should like to read of all the Earthly news, perhaps enjoy the magazines. And so, to the spaceman he would casually say, in a most unruffled manner: "Paper, mister?"

But there was no ship or spaceman, no customers at all at this hour; no one to hear him mutter as he had so many times to himself, with each passing shadow, "Paper?"

Lonely here, thought the old newsy huddled under yellow light with his night phantoms, but, he pondered as he turned his gaze to the stars in the dark, it's lonelier up there, I'll bet. Lonelier up there.

AN ATTEMPT AT INCLUSION

Who can hope to present an all inclusive consideration as to what might be *the* most salient aspects of the Universe critical to our most basically comprehensive understanding of that overwhelming…*body*? Arrogantly, we shall, with appropriate apologies, attempt this, with the initial notice that we shall inescapably ultimately provide some contention with a few "universally" apparently accepted notions, but shall also hope to contribute a modicum of compensating awareness amidst those who may have entertained some meditative thought to this cosmological area.

Skirting the more intricate, profound and complex disciplines of quantum mechanics and particle physics we shall attempt to approach an understanding of our place in time and space with the consideration of seven basic, essential, components that generally, and in a large way, comprise what we sense as all embracing concepts. These basics are fundamental to any further "cosmic" understanding, while avoiding possible misconceptions, of *where* we are, and to where, if there is a "where" we might be headed.

Here are the major elements aside from particles and fields, gravity, dark matter, dark energy as well as the several paradoxes and conundrums of particle physics (such as "entanglement" where detached elements can bear influence on one another and convey information to one another despite vast distance):

Distance…Time…Space…Shape…Size…Speed…Number.

Distances contained within our Universe are so vast, no number or concept can embrace them…. Consider that these "distances" constitute ALL the distances that exist. (Save the speculative additional "bubble" or "multi"- universes.) And it should be noted that these distances in space extend FROM EVERY point. Generally, when one thinks of some infinite extension or projection, one's thinking might protract or stretch out before one…in one direction. But also imagine an exact, infinite extension going in …every one of at least four directions as well as up…and down! Simply put, infinity would extend behind us as well as below, above and on all four opposing sides of us and not simply toward only one direction.

This may, on examination, sound simplistic but is rarely ever noted, and eventually common thinking and consideration is linear, rarely envisioning the infinite distances which might comprise a more spherical projection rather than"one infinity," extending only in one direction. This important notation has significant bearing on the expansion of the Universe and where it might be headed!

Related to the concept of Distance, is Time, as well as Space. The common problem is the question of finite or infinite…and also, oddly, the question of Shape. But which element should logically be considered first, if there is such a thing as a relative order here? Let us consider Time.

As well as Space, Time, in covering the concept of Distance, will also be consumed. And, if the Distance and medium of Space prove to be *infinite*, Time will be as well and Time, like Distance, will cease to be meaningful or calculable at all. (Keep this in mind as we consider Space.) Time will be so extended in such a void as to have nothing (no thing) to chronicle…no change to record…no starting or ending points to measure or to render anything of any duration meaningful. Duration because of infinite length (in any direction) loses meaning. At last, as Distance and Space doubles back on itself, so will Time, at which point there will be nothing against which to measure itself. And the element of Time, will likewise prove to be spherical!

Space is not a void…but comprises much of what we have only suggested earlier, and what is accepted and assumed to fill it (though whose constituents are not fully understood). The important and relevant notion is that Space is not "nothing".

"Nothing" is what lies outside of, beyond, Space. Space will extend in all directions, to "double" (or quadruple) back on itself, four dimensionally, just as the sphere of the Earth analogously comes back around on itself. There is no "rim," no "edge"…. It is only more Space "doubling" back upon itself to more Space.... "Outside" of itself there is "nothing." This is the finite nature of Space and the Universe! It occurs at the end of immense extensiveness of unimaginable, but finite, boundaries. There IS NO "infinite"…only an immense finite four-dimensional doubling (or quadrupling) back on itself of Space…beyond which is simply…Nothing! No void…no blackness… no vacuum…no space….no emptiness…Nothing!

In our brief discussion of Space we have inadvertently alluded to Shape. A story meant to be amusing is told where a physicist is called upon to solve a problem. He begins by drawing a circle…a sphere. There is good reason for this. The two dimensional circle or the three dimensional sphere is basic…to almost everything. It is enveloping. It is fundamental. From the proton and the neutron to planets, immense stars, galaxies, galactic clusters and the Universe, the sphere is more than an initial foundation, it is an entirety. And although cosmologists deem the Universe to be "flat"…(not in the two, but in the three dimensional form and not concave or ovoid) we posit it is… a sphere…albeit in four dimensions. Simply, it is…eventually… round…!

For added perspective, we should not neglect to mention Size. This relative concept can tend to lose its abstract character and singular identity when witnessed in its diverse forms. Compare almost anything in human experience with the Size of a star whose diameter is so broad that it would take more than one thousand years to jet across it; many, many, lifetimes to speed from one end of this star to its other side. The Size of such a gargantuan creation might well be perceived by the participant witness flyer to be…infinite…and the journey across, forever!

But the abstract concept of Size, of the particle, or of this "forever" giant, is the same. It is incomprehensibly, apparently, limitless. The Universe has immense, though most likely finite, Size. And, again with limited comprehension, Size "extends" itself as vastly toward the unendingly diminishing, microscopic, realms as well as the seemingly infinite, macroscopic, Universe.

There, may however, be hidden dimensions at this microscopic level. As a cable strung one hundred yards from us *appears* to present only the <u>one dimension</u> of length, we can observe its second and third dimensions of width and depth as we approach more closely. So it is, on the, so far, unexaminable dimensions on the sub-particle plane, where additional dimensions are theorized to exist, folded in on themselves, hidden from our observation.

Speed, on its cosmic scale is equally challenging to the imagination within our limited experience. We know the speed of massless light photons but can we <u>comprehend</u> 186,000 miles per – second (even if this is thought to be a cosmic speed "limit!")? If the Earth is eight thousand miles around light could circumvent the planet some 24 times in only one second. This is truly unfathomable but is this extraordinary Speed, which takes 4.4 million years for light to travel to or from our nearest star and has taken billions of years for light to traverse our visible Universe, the <u>ultimate</u> Speed?

Since it has been discovered that Space itself is expanding, and the galactic bodies within are flying apart from one another at enormous and constantly <u>increasing</u> rates, our cosmic "Speed Limit" seems to have been left behind! New speeds at beyond the speed of light have been calculated. What this would seem to indicate is that <u>there is no speed limit</u>…and, in fact, the very concept of limit, in our Universe, does not exist!

In its close relation to Time we could add one final observation: Einstein has posited, and it has been documented, that one's clock,

"Time" itself, slows as the Speed of light is approached by the traveler. At perhaps twice the Speed of light (or even less) clocks might stop altogether. Distances would be traversed instantly…as Time would not exist! To illustrate, if not confirm this odd notion, there are high energy particles called muons, which are produced at extremely high altitudes in space. The lifetime of a muon is so brief that even if a muon were to travel at the speed of light it could not reach Earth before decaying. Inexplicably, however, recent experiments have shown a constant flux of muons paradoxically reaching the Earth…from the cosmos, and beyond the "time" of what is known to be their life expectancy! How can this be? The answer, it is theorized, is that muons live longer in our frame of reference than in their own and can therefore reach Earth…at their light speed…as our clocks amble on…relative to us. The faster one travels…the slower one's own clock advances. Time slows for the traveler…and can, apparently, approach zero…perhaps even move backward in Time!

Finally we comment on the one essential concept that would appear to stand alone. It does so in that as Space and Distance, Space and Time, Space and Shape, Space and Size, Space and Speed, Size and Shape, Time and Speed, Time and Distance are related, Number, or in this case multiples of mass, seems to, ironically, in a manner of speaking, stand alone. Perhaps this is because of its very essence. But Number is NOT alone! The Number of un-imaginably sized stars in the Universe out-numbers the number of grains of sand on all the beaches of our planet. The Number of stars in our galaxy is in the hundreds of billions…. And the number of galaxies is in the billions! Distances of light years and time separate most of the bodies! The concept of Number is only seen attempting to approach and fill Distance and Space, with whatever Shape or Size, in however much Time and with whatever Speed… but it fails! The Number of objects cannot compete with Space, Distance and Time, and as a concept, perhaps with, but undaunted by, Size, stands alone!

A problem to refute any attempted clarification above is posed by Alan Guth's "Inflation" theory, i.e. how could the Inflationary creation event, of such ostensible magnitude, occur on its immense scale without having a central starting point albeit however briefly? How could the "bang" of inflation occur ALL AT ONCE —no central point-… (Time/ Speed)…EVERYWHERE -no central point-…(Space/Distance)? And, paradoxically, if Inflation, conversely DID occur (initially) at one central point, traversing the boundaries and limits of Space/Distance… how did it then ARRIVE at the now, FINALLY visible point 13.8 billion light years *from* us…faster than light (instantly?) which has taken 13.8 billion years for its light to have, now, finally reached us? (At the Cosmic Speed Limit!)

At the quantum level, causes of events cannot be accurately determined, in fact, often they cannot be discerned or even observed. Quantum events seem to come into existence on a probability grid…and exist amidst an array of probabilities. So, CAN effects, outcomes, on the sub-atomic level have NO CAUSE? And, do particles… perhaps the entire Universe…have their own, self contained clocks…and follow their own probability schedules…independent of outside "cause?"

There are more than a few cosmological theories as to the origins of the Universe but there is one favorite of mine. It states that WHEN it is discovered just how and why the Universe exists…the Universe will vanish…and will be replaced with an exact duplicate.

There is another theory which states this has ALREADY OCCURRED!

SHIPWRECK

My name is Lyle Kitchener. I'm 380. I've been on this ship…this…thing, ever since I can remember. And I'll be the last one. We, my shipmates and I, my fellow humans, were the only ones to venture forth…and now there is no one left. So, I'm setting it all down. To no point…no end, really; but I'm a chronicler…a recorder.

It was foolish, in a way, ever to embark on this project but, I am supposing, we had to do it. It's in the human spirit, is it not? Curiosity…the quests…the need to, as Browning said, reach! "What's a heaven for?" And, exceed our grasp, we did.

The journey began several thousand years ago, I don't recall exactly how many the initial crew comprised; the records were burned, data banks in our computers, destroyed. But lives, generations, were spent on this very tub…this awesome, startling, creation. Our library rooms alone are daunting by virtue of their very physical size. We were self sustaining. We grew our food, procreated, educated our own and learned. We evolved. And we suffered. And now….

Did I mention we were a fleet? Yes, we were. Masters of the galaxies. We were the lords of the Universe. So we thought.

The idea was to take ourselves through our destiny…to the rim, the outer edge, *the* limits of this house. The ultimate object was to find a new home, a hospitable one, one which would accommodate us as the advanced civilization we had become. Of course, it was not to be an easy task, but allow me to explain first what I mean by "advanced civilization."

It has long been posited by physicists, specifically one Nikolai Kardashev, in the mid nineteen hundreds (centuries ago) that essentially three, perhaps four, classes of civilizations exist. Type A is the first advanced class, having mastered its environment, conquered disease with a complete understanding of medicine, social problems, food distribution, basic physical and chemical technology, meteorology. In a Type A there is no more war, hunger, blight, no more crime, droughts, floods, fires, hurricanes, turmoil. Human age is on its way to becoming limitless. The oceans are tamed, explored, exploited. It is Eden, again. But this is not an end. It is a beginning; for the forces of a larger and more formidable solar system exist "outside" and loom inexorably.

The Type B civilization is equipped to deal with this, our solar system. Type B has conquered space and the neighboring planets. It has harnessed the power and energies of its life-giving star and is ready, after thousands of years, to achieve, the physicist's dream: the realization, and bringing to bear the fulfillment, of Type C...a civilization in possession and in command of vast stores of knowledge, of a complete chemistry, of a complete physics; skilled in the application of all its laws, and destined to reach beyond the galaxies...virtually, as the poet would say, beyond the stars! The energy for this will not come from the civilization's home planet, nor its sun, but from any of the billions of stars in its universe. Type C is quite independent! So we thought.

Earth attained Type A status in the year 2300...almost predictably. The achievement of Type B was agonizingly slower and did not occur for some three thousand years afterward. So far as I know, Type C has not been reached, and may never be reached (the anticipated gap between a Type B and Type C takes a geometric leap, and is upwards of 500,000 years) and to my knowledge, as I write this, Earth itself is long gone. We embraced our exploratory mission prematurely and in haste.

Those who began this mission did so in extreme faith and commitment; always a danger, but necessary. Those departing the home planet knew they would never be returning, not in physical body.

There were incentives, however, and, as in all such ventures, there was excitement and the lure of the unknown. Additionally our early voyagers were old. They had enjoyed the equivalent of many lifetimes on Earth. And some felt they were going home.

Life aboard the MESSENGER was almost normal. The ship was stocked with every possible provision, built to afford every conceivable luxury and convenience, including numerous theaters, gardens, libraries, schools, gymnasiums and parks. We even had an onboard lake and a football stadium. Soon, incredibly, we had a wonderful museum. A fleet of adjacent and trailing sister ships carried nothing more than streets and boulevards accessible to all. The difference was we were moving...and at enormous rates of speed.

We had no indication of what shall to this day still be referred to as the dark matter.... It was some kind of radiation belt we cut through for which the ship had had no protection. The field sliced through our many mainframes with no apparent damage other than destroying hundreds of data banks of records and technical material. We never knew quite what we had encountered.

And then the fires started. There was no apparent reason for them but they erupted with no warning and carried a unique fury that was, although violent and frequent, short lived...but destructive. And then there were the event horizons which we, through good fortune, narrowly evaded but whose immense pull and ruinous forces took a formidable toll. Again, data banks were destroyed, sensitive calibrations ravaged, and delicate magnetic settings, that determined our course, thrown hopelessly out of kilter.

The rates of speed at which we traveled were exceeded by factors which, to our surprise, were difficult to measure. But at nearly ten percent the velocity of light strange variations in speed began to occur. Again, inexplicable. It was as if the ship were suddenly going...downhill; an ever accelerating free fall.

When the speeds increased and approached those of light, which we thought were absolute, we were aware of our body clocks (and all clocks aboard ship) slowing considerably. What to anyone earthbound would have been years were only minutes, if not less, to us. A few hours or days to anyone aboard our ship were years, even millennia, to those back home. Primarily we knew this by our reckoning and the constellations and stars we were passing. They were hundreds of light years away, yet we were navigating them in ostensibly far less time. Compared to us the rest of the universe was whizzing past us...to where we had just been!

Wherever we were going, it appeared that we would get there sooner than anyone had imagined…and yet we seemed also to be going nowhere. We had passed an outpost beyond our local neighborhood of galaxies, the Virgo Cluster…some 60 million light years from where we started a mere few thousand years back…and the quasars. And, evidently at an ever increasing rate of speed, we appeared to be going…nowhere now. We saw and passed nothing.

It was shortly thereafter, looking back at a fading Virgo, that, I recall… people began to die. They were mysterious deaths, like the half life of radioactive particles, brought about by nothing, arrested by nothing. And the bodies disintegrated. Vanished. I, however, was unaffected.

Our sister fleet fell behind into oblivion as well. One had apparently never made it beyond the particularly powerful and devastating event horizon of an invisible black hole. Only MESSENGER was left…with me at the helm...somehow invincible, but without apparent purpose.

It has been days now, by my clock, weeks…for you, perhaps eons. I know the speed of the ship is vacillating. The instruments do not hold steady. I think she is picking up speed…if that is possible, but it is no longer possible to slow the ship. The retro rockets are long gone; the magnets have no potency; there is nothing against which we can repel this incomprehensibly accelerating momentum and movement…in whatever direction we are facing. My last hope lies in perhaps hitting some dark matter. But where that is and how it presents itself always has been, and, I think, forever will be, an enigma. Chances of slowing, even imperceptibly, seem slim.

I could leave a date but it seems pointless. Time has lost meaning to me. Suffice it to say I've not recorded any of these strange events for what, might be some days. The void that I can recall since passing the Virgo Cluster has been depressing and debilitating, and has sapped my strength but yesterday for several hours I noted a bright flicker deep in the blackness ahead of the ship. It carries some hope, but it is puzzling because as of late, any flicker, any star before us, shifted from blue to red as we neared it at speeds approaching that of light and as we watched it recede.

No star, no galaxy, no light remained positioned before us, and our meteoric approach, for this length of time. Either the ship was slowing or this object was traveling faster than we were…hardly a possibility, or it was too far away to comprehend or… something else!

One of the pieces of equipment aboard still in excellent functioning order was an old Hubble scope. It was optically many times superior to the early versions but still bore the proud name, Hubble. A prized feature of this model was its ability to determine the age of the light it reflected into the eyepiece. Was it five hundred year old light…and that many years away? Was it only one light year away? It revealed whether the sighted object, indeed, existed at all…or was it merely the target's old, long reflected, light one was looking at.

Focusing on the object, a light flicker was noticeable and also a change in the red shift. The ship and I were gaining on it ever so slightly. But there was something very strange about the image. For anything to be so far from us, its light was very young. At our rate of approaching speed, this object had to be light years away (lest we would soon be upon it and passing it)…its light would have to be several years old…yet it was not. And the Hubble also measured its size as incredibly small.

For days there was little change in the object as we closed in on it. It almost appeared to be racing along with us through the ebony ether. The red shift, however, was becoming distinctly bluer. And our speed kept increasing…uncontrollably.

186,000 miles per second is not merely the speed of light. It has been thought to be the *absolute* speed at which anything can travel. Light travels at *this* speed because light travels at the supposed fastest speed possible in this universe. Or so we thought. But we had neared this speed weeks ago when the braking systems failed. Our clocks slowed to almost no movement as our acceleration continued. Time had almost come to a halt for us as we coursed through infinity. As we approached the velocity of light, we were, in effect, traveling back *through* time, meeting light given off from stars and galaxies years and eons before. And if we were to surpass that "absolute" speed, we would overtake the light that shone upon all our histories…old light…that had not reached a final destination. Turning behind us, we could see history…; we could see ourselves taking off!

If all this were not bizarre enough, the inexplicable occurred. What was left of our navigation monitors began showing our passage of constellations and nebulae, galaxies and clusters long since passed. Brilliant orange Arcturus in Bootes, no longer in the Milky Way, became visible once more, Deneb, the tail of Cygnus, initially some fifteen hundred light years away at the start of our journey went whizzing past. Rigel, at 850 light years distant at our voyage's onset, the great star in Orion, momentarily flared and lit the surrounding dark sky. All a vast blur, the Milky Way, Andromeda, Fornax, The Magellenic Clouds and finally The Virgo Cluster and the quasars appeared, as if in the recap of a dream, then vanished. And the light, the mysterious flicker before us never left our screen.

At first I disassembled the equipment, finding nothing. The image persisted.

And our speed increased.

Today, my last day, I have finally understood. It is good this will finally be over. Nothing can exceed and defy the laws of the universe. Nothing can break the boundaries that confine us.

At last I have fathomed why the object before us never wavered. I now knew why its light was young, why it never shifted from blue to red, why, a constant companion to this ship, it never receded before us.... The object was not traveling faster than we were. We were not slowing. If anything we were traveling faster that the light...the gleam, and its source. I realized too late we would soon be upon it. And I could not slow the ship nor alter is course. As we passed Virgo and the quasars for the final time, and closed upon the object, I understood.

The Universe is curved...a great globe of curved space. Countless trillions of miles...light years...but finite nonetheless...curved! We've been circling! It's taken thousands of years, but we've gone in one, nearly infinite, circle...until recently. The speeds our ship attained broke absolute velocity and subsequently all physical law. I don't know the final speeds we achieved. *We passed ourselves. We left ourselves behind!* The MESSENGER had attained a velocity which enabled the ship to pass everything that comprised it...everything that constituted its identity.... It passed itself, and in doing so, breaking through the barriers of time, unable to slow, is about to crash into itself, like a dog finally catching its tail. That floating mass of apparent detritus before us is the MESSENGER! She still travels at near light speed, but appears, to us, a derelict MESSENGER. We had broken all boundaries of space...and now Time, as well. I cannot slow the ship at these speeds. We are about to collide with the ship we have passed. We have doubled back upon ourselves and are about to collide with ourselves... with Time itself!

I, Lyle Kitchener, captain of the MESSENGER, have reached the end of this voyage. And my ship, at her final speeds, has caught up with, and is momentarily about to overtake, Time. And Time… has caught up with the MESSENGER.

Old ideas like old habits die slowly. The speed at which a bullet travels could no longer be considered awesome, yet the Constellation Train that made the Orion run, up through the Milky Way through Gemini, to the Great Square in Pegasus was called The Bullet. It carried the name proudly even though it would take a bullet (at bullet speed) more than several million years to reach places the Train would arrive at in just hours today. The name simply persisted. Perhaps it was the old idea.

Now, how does one travel to the farthest constellations in such a short time? Part of the answer lies in refraction. Things are not always where we suppose them to be. Light bends. Space curves. Our universe is unbounded...but it is finite. It doubles back upon itself. Lines emanating from a point can end exactly where they began even though they progress in a forward direction and make no angular turns. Like advancing on a sphere or Mobius strip: one surface doubling back on itself, one side and one edge...or no sides...no edges.

And because distant stars move by the time their light even reaches us, their images appear to be where things are not. And not only are these things not where they are supposed to be...they could be anywhere. They could be everywhere. The trick, then, is to put the traveler there too.

COSTELLATION STATION

Karl opened the book of maps. Inside, however, there were no maps. There seemed to be…a story! It began: "Through his room window, Karl could see the night was thick, but he could see pinpoints of gold and patches of orange light scattered along the horizon. Soon, thought Karl, he would reach Constellation Station. He had been planning this trip for as long as he could remember and now, finally, his dream would become realized. In his leather bag Karl had packed everything he would need: spare clothing, food provisions, books, star maps, a flashlight, a pair of pocket binoculars and writing materials. He also took a few silver coins, some fine silk pocket squares, a small flask of excellent cola, and a modest amount of his favorite, subtle, cologne. To compliment the cola, Karl also remembered to take a bag of wonderful deep fried, spicy vegetable chips and a pocket knife with several blades for any occasion.

"In the distance, not too far from the horizon, there was a clearing beyond the trees. Every so often it would appear when the road crested. Then, as Karl jogged down from the summit, this clearing would vanish from sight. When it appeared once again Karl could make out the toasty building surrounded by trees. It was lit from the inside and had big, beautiful brass letters atop the entrance. The words read: CONSTELLATION STATION. He was almost there.

"The man who stood with his arms folded across his vested chest looked at Karl as he approached toting his neatly clasped and very professional-looking bag. He watched the young man huffing his way up the final slope and then consulted his pocket watch. It was a time honored gesture which comprised the essence of conductors whether they ran trains terrestrial or extra-terrestrial. It was an especially large watch with a clear glass face through which all the gears and workings of the watch were visible. On the other side of the timepiece, as Karl would later observe, was a pocket barometer, equally useless where the Constellation Train was going.

"Ten minutes to departure, son," said the conductor. His rather excessive midsection pushed hard against the golden buttons on his vest. They looked as if they might burst.

"I'm coming," said Karl. His breath was short. "How far inside before I get to the train?"

"Not far," said the man as he replaced his gleaming watch after solidly snapping the lid shut. "Just follow me."

"And so the two of them, the conductor a good foot and a half taller than Karl, hurried toward the great Constellation Train somewhere inside the station. They walked through a large vestibule, a smaller waiting room, traversed a short hallway, passed beneath a lofty great arch and beheld, in all her quiet but powerful majesty, the awesome and nearly blinding gleam of the Bullet. It was difficult to determine if her brilliant gleam was silvery or gold. Just like the sun, thought Karl. Equally difficult to ascertain was her height. But she was at least several stories tall and streamlined from every direction as far as the eye could see. From where Karl stood he could not see as far as the locomotive. Nor could he discern the top of the train or the last of her cars. The Bullet was enveloped in bright light and boundlessness. It was as if she encroached into or onto our plane from a higher, four dimensional space. She seemed not to be rooted, even seated, in the Constellation Station whatsoever. To Karl, she was the night train of night trains! Bullet to adventure, darkness and the unknown.

"The shimmering doors melted open, noiselessly, and with no apparent motion. "Aboard," said the conductor. "All aboard!"

"Karl picked up his leather bag, which he had a moment ago reluctantly put down, and stepped aboard the Bullet. The movement seemed effortless. Before him, where a moment before Karl had seen, or had simply assumed was, the other side of the train, there appeared to be a lengthy corridor. About six or eight doors down on his left stood the pot-bellied conductor. As Karl approached him he noticed the man was standing at the very place from which Karl had boarded seconds ago.

"You forgot your ticket," the conductor said, handing Karl a beautiful 3x5 hologram of the constellations. "And you will be getting off at…?" He paused.

"I'll be going as far as Arcturus in Bootes today" (although the visit to Arcturus was actually scheduled for tomorrow). "On the way back I'd like to stop at the Pleiades."

"Very good," said the conductor. "That will be twelve fifty."

"Karl peeled off the twelve fifty from a small packet of bills he withdrew from his pocket.

"You're in room 601," said the man. "Down the corridor and on your right."

"Taking note of the room on his right from where he stood, Karl glanced at the compartments at the end of the long car and quickly estimated how far he would have to go before reaching 601. The finish on the door had a strange iridescent shimmer which defied focusing on any part of it. The digits themselves seemed to come and go. A big wall clock over the portal read a few minutes before 8 o'clock.

"The compartment itself was pleasant and roomier than Karl would have anticipated. One entire side of the room was clear glass with two generous bunk beds that folded into seating accommodations. This was to Karl's right as he faced the big side window. To Karl's left were 2 doors at the front of the compartment.

"Karl was not able to see very clearly out of the side window as it was quite dark outside, on the platform of the train station. His attention was drawn to the doors to his left. Opening one of them, Karl discovered it to be only the small lavatory for the compartment. And then, something very strange happened. Opening the second door, Karl for a long moment thought he had somehow turned himself around inadvertently, as he was peering down the very corridor from which he had just entered! That was not the case, however, as a quick glance about revealed. Karl wondered if he might have stumbled on another passageway on the train, accessed from his room. This might have been a possibility except that, first of all, the corridors were perpendicular to one another! And everyone knows trains are straight and have no perpendicular corridors. Second, the passageways appeared to be identical. Looking out from either one of the doors, (which were at ninety degrees to one another) Karl found himself looking across the passage at room 600. It was directly in front of him. As Karl was about to step back into his strange room he noticed something else. The large clock hanging outside, above and to the right of his cabin, read 1 o'clock. He stepped back inside and closed the door. It was not 1 o'clock. The luminous hands on Karl's watch were coming up on 8 o'clock! He rushed to the other door from which he had gained entry to his compartment and opened it. The wall clock outside read, as his watch indicated, 8 o'clock.

"Aboard!" shouted the pot-bellied conductor as he looked both ways while standing on the metal steps at the rear of the car. Steam gushed from somewhere and seemed to fill the station. A whistle blew and Karl could hear the sound of the great wheels beneath the Bullet. Peering through the side windows he could not detect any motion, but could feel the vibration around him as the train, Karl somehow knew, was leaving Constellation Station. As he closed his compartment door Karl noticed a neatly printed page posted on it. It said: DOOR A - STANDARD TIME. Karl turned to the other portal. It read:

DOOR B - CAUTION - LIGHT YEARS: 200.

"Beneath that, in smaller print, the poster went on:

MULTIPLES OF 200 LY FOR EACH CORRIDOR TRAVERSED. ENTER THROUGH COMPARTMENT 600 (DOOR A). EXIT THROUGH DOOR B TO ADD 200 LY. TO CONTINUE TO ADD, ENTER A OF 600, EXIT B. TO SUBTRACT, RETURN THROUGH B OF 600, THEN A... DISTANCE IN LY WILL ALWAYS BE 200 TIMES THE NUMBER OF B DOORS EXITED. SHOULD YOU LOSE TRACK, CONSULT THE CORRIDOR CLOCK. IT WILL TELL YOU HOW MANY B DOORS YOU HAVE GONE THROUGH. MULTIPLY THIS BY 200 AND YOU WILL KNOW HOW MANY LIGHT YEARS YOU HAVE TRAVELED. REMEMBER: <u>TO RETRACE</u> MORE THAN 200 LY, YOU MUST GO THROUGH A B DOOR OF THE OPPOSITE COMPARTMENT (EITHER 600 OR 601). <u>TO ADVANCE</u> IN <u>MULTIPLES OF TEN,</u> MOVE CLOCK FORWARD ONE HOUR. TO RETURN, MOVE CLOCK BACK. GOOD LUCK!

"Karl consulted the itinerary which he carried in his inside jacket pocket. "Let's see," he thought, "Orion ought to be coming up pretty soon. And that's certainly one I don't want to miss." He stared at his watch, then at the two passageway doors in his room. Outside, through the compartment's window, Karl could see specks of blue and glittery light. The door opened. It was the conductor.

"Don't worry about the clocks, son, I'll be taking care of them for you. But don't be wandering through Room 600. We don't want you getting lost!"

"The last thing Karl needed was to be getting lost through Room 600.

"But you did want to see Orion, I hope," said the conductor.

"Absolutely," said Karl. "But will there be dinner first?"

"Yes, indeed," said the conductor, "We'll be eating on Betelgeuse, at Orion's right shoulder. Dining at Rigel, Orion's left leg would be quite something, but I'm afraid it's so bright the ambience would hardly be conducive to a pleasant repast. You see, Rigel is about 60,000 times as bright as looking directly into our sun. It isn't called the Cosmic Searchlight for nothing. If it were any closer to us we would have no nighttime at all. Not very romantic for dinner. No, sir. But don't worry. That's why we're headed for Betelgeuse. She's the biggest single object you can see in our universe with your naked eye. And she IS big. About 800 times as big as the sun. Nonetheless," added the conductor, "she's far enough away to give us some privacy, about 500 light years from here. Don't worry," he chuckled, "I'll take care of the clocks!"

"As the conductor adjusted his cap and backed out into the hallway, Karl seated himself on the overstuffed easy chair by his window and watched as the stars and constellations swept by. He had his nose pressed up against the large glass, watching a huge orange star grow larger and larger, until it filled his entire field of view, when a voice chimed over the train's speakers:

"Orion dinner is now being served in the main dining car....Please exit through the "A" portal to your left. For those visiting Cygnus, breakfast is served, also in the main dining car, through the B portal on your right."

"In the main dining car, Karl met a bountiful array of sandwiches, fried potatoes and beverages. For desert there were cakes, fruit pies and frosted crèmes. And then a booming voice filled the train:

"Welcome to Orion," it said. "I am one of the largest and most prominent constellations in the winter sky. My alpha star is beautiful, orange, Betelgeuse, the largest star, the largest single object, that you can see in the heavens with the naked eye. My pride, is brilliant, blue, Rigel, a giant among suns. The three stars across my belt, Alnilam, Alnitak and Mintaka are thousands of light years apart, and thousands of years beyond us, but still, members of our family. The others include

Bellatrix and Saiph, and if you look closely you can see my sword, inside of which resides the Orion Nebula, stretching for some 30 light years across, and more than 1500 light years from here. The brightest center and the nucleus of all these molecules and gases are four stars known as the Trapezeum. And above all of this, just below my belt, is the famous, dark and mysterious Horsehead Nebula, standing about one light year high. Traveling at the absolute speed, the speed of light, 186,000 miles in one second…it would take more than one year to reach bottom from here! That's a deep, deep hole!" Orion spoke in a loud, powerful, reverberating voice. "Beneath me is Lepus the rabbit," he continued, "and flowing off below and to my left is the strange cosmic river Eridanus, as she flows south and into the other side of the universe!" Karl looked about and studied the great majesty of Orion. There was a pause and then the voice continued. "Higher in the heavens, and just beyond my left shoulder is my eternal quarry, Taurus the Bull, with his mysterious and beautiful Hyades and Pleiades, two moving clusters of brilliant stars. I am power and strength. Indefatigable and eternal. I will watch over you, guide you and protect you. Watch for me. I am the Hunter, master of the winter skies, Orion!" There was an awed silence in the dining car as everyone pondered the words of Orion and studied the great constellation. The quiet lasted for several seconds before the clinking of silverware and the chiming of china resumed.

"Karl finished several sandwiches and embarked on an orange and lime crème as the Bullet shot down beyond Betelgeuse, across the Trapezeum and into the strange Horsehead Nebula. Everything suddenly became extremely dark and quiet as time itself seemed to stop. Then a voice said: "Ladies and gentlemen, we hope you enjoyed your dinner tonight. Our next stop will be the summer triangle of stars in the constellations Cygnus, Lyra and Aquila. Our first stop will be Cygnus, the Swan, at seven a.m. breakfast. For those of you staying here in our main dining car for the remainder of this evening, we will be passing through Gemini, the Twins, shortly, and then on to Auriga. Tea will be served and there will be a light snack.

"Karl decided he had seen enough for one evening, felt tired, and thought he might need his rest for the Summer Triangle tomorrow morning. So he got up, tucked his chair under the table, and headed back to his compartment.

"The night was filled with dreams as Karl lay on his bunk bed, gazing out at the starriness. There was no longer night or day as we know it to be, only a vast, black-bathed, starriness. Karl scanned his star maps and tried to discern some of the constellations, but from his vantage point it seemed impossible. It was as if someone had taken the parts, the stars and galaxies and nebulae of which they were made, rearranged them, and scattered them about. His thoughts melted into the speckled darkness, thoughts of the great constellations, and the morning brightened by the suns of Cygnus and Lyra, and he fell asleep.

"Karl was awakened by a gentle sounding bell and a knock at his compartment door.

"Good morning," said the recognizable voice of the rotund conductor. "Breakfast will be at 7, Cygnus at 7:30."

"Karl washed and dressed, took his best binoculars, and was seated for breakfast in the dining car over pancakes and bacon before he knew it. At 7:30 everyone was invited into the Bullet's observation car which was constructed completely and seamlessly of Steuben glass. For several moments, silence pervaded the car and then all lights were dimmed as the great swan, Cygnus took shape and came into view.

"Good morning," she said. I am Cygnus, the Swan. I am grace and serenity. I fly high over your summers with my companions, Lyra, the Harp and the soaring Aquila, the Eagle, to form the great summer triangle which can be seen extending over your entire northern hemisphere. My length spans from the double star Albireo at my head, to my alpha star, Deneb, one of the sky's most magnificent supergiants among stars, at my tail. Albireo is a scant 380 light years from the earth, while Deneb, with a diameter larger than 60 of your suns, and brighter than 60,000 of them, is more than 1600 light years away. Alas, between my head and tail there stretches more than 1200 light years! So, it is no wonder that despite his luminosity and size, Deneb, second perhaps in awesome brightness only to the blue giant Rigel, in Orion, appears to be the faintest in our summer triangle. For Lyra's Vega is 26 light years away, and Aquila's Altair is only 16 light years from the Earth." Everyone gasped, as Karl pondered the vast discrepancy of distances which, nonetheless, had managed to form, and so clearly reveal, this heavenly alliance. "To the left of Deneb," Cygnus continued, "is the North America nebula. From here, it may look only like a hazy cloud, for it lies some 2700 light years away, but its shape is strangely, exactly, like the continent of North America. It is larger than that, however. Its actual diameter, from "coast to coast," is 100 light years. And, I might add, nearly all my stars lie amid the riches of the Milky Way, our galaxy, and have no want of light or companionship. So what we share with you is the same: light, grace, friendships and joy. And beneath our canopy of the great summer triangle the lesson that, despite distance and difference, the linking of grace, beauty and power, that great connection, can be made and discerned and can become one." Karl looked through the dome of the great observation car, through the seamless, almost invisible glass, as the constellation Cygnus, the Swan, seemed to fly away into the heavens and disappear into the infinite expanse.

"There is more, ladies and gentlemen," said a voice, "if you look left, you will see the beautiful constellation Lyra." Everyone gasped as they turned. It was the most beautiful constellation Karl had ever seen. The closeness, the elegant majesty, the gold immensity and symmetry of the harp and the somehow eloquent brilliance of the great star Vega, fourth brightest in the sky, was more than captivating. It was stunning. In its simplicity, it was complex. Karl knew he could never tire of this sight and would never forget it. Lyra had always commanded interest from his perch behind his house on Earth, but here, in its overwhelming dimension, Lyra outshone everything he had ever known. Karl could almost hear her music. Her presence was commanding. Inside the observation car there was complete and utter silence. Somehow, there seemed to be little need for any sound. The vision of Lyra was eloquent enough. But then, there was a sound. Karl had never heard anything quite like before. It was faint, yet clear and overpowering. It was completely and fully harmonic. It was soft and unimposing. Then the voice of Lyra. Karl knew. It seemed to come from within.

"I am Lyra," said the lovely voice. "I am comfort, beauty, truth! John Keats said it. Beauty is truth, truth beauty. All you know on Earth, all you need to know. Look to me in the fullness of summer, think of me, so far away, as I look across the skies to you. Think of me in winter when you can no longer see me, but listen and hope, and wait, and we will meet again. We will not lose each other." Suddenly Karl was aware of Vega herself and saw the illusion. She was not gold as the rest of the constellation had at first appeared to be, but a lovely, definite, blue. He knew, too, he would never forget her, and would, no matter where he was, look for her always.

"As the music grew fainter and Lyra became small and distant, the quiet was broken by the familiar voice of the conductor.

"And on your right, ladies and gentlemen, behold, Aquila the Eagle."

"It was thrilling to see; prominent and defined; like a giant kite…like…an Eagle!

"My grand star Altair, the third member of the summer triangle, is only some ten times as bright as your sun. Hardly the 60,000 times boasted by Deneb in Cygnus. But we have come millions of light years over time and we have endurance and proximity. We boast closeness and staying power. See the power of the Eagle, his brightness! See him soar. Take comfort in that when you see him in the heavens. There is not the beauty of Lyra but there is the pride, power and strength of the Eagle. Aquila, the Eagle sees you!"

"Lunch is served," said a voice on the loudspeaker. And Karl, joined by starry-eyed companions, filed dreamily into the brightly lit dining car.

"After a fine lunch of sandwiches, complimented by some of Karl's spicy vegetable chips, cole slaw and soda, Karl, still munching the last of an orange-icing cupcake, stole off to his compartment to contemplate what he had experienced that morning, joyfully anticipating the late afternoon's meeting with the great constellation, Bootes, the Herdsman. Space, as seen through his window, speckled and streaked with galaxies and stars, blues, yellows, oranges and whites, seemed infinite. How could it be, thought Karl, that this went on forever and ever? And if there was an end to it, what was there at its end, a wall? And what would there be beyond that? Karl peered out at the infinite darkness and thought about it. Then, suddenly, he knew! Just as in Columbus's time it appeared impossible to imagine someone in front of you, setting off on a straight line journey to eventually arrive behind you, so it seems now impossible to think of a space ship soaring off on a straight course, eventually arriving exactly where it began! But, just as the two dimensional plane of the Earth is curved, so is the three dimensional plane of space curved. As all points on a straight line on Earth lead back to themselves, so do all points on a straight line in curved space fall back on themselves. You keep going…farther and farther out…but you arrive back at your starting point. There is no wall…there is no end! Space simply doubles back on itself. It is finite, but in its vast curvature, at the same time, infinite. Of course it would take a very, very long time…but there you have it.

"Then, settling back, Karl thought about Bootes. Ever since he first began reading about the stars, and the skies, and the constellations, he remembered seeing the name: Bootes. At first he pronounced it Boots…as in cowboy…or Booties as in baby shoes…or, on seeing its often used abbreviation, just Boo, as in ghost. But then he learned it was pronounced Boh-oh-tees. It was mentioned in nearly all of Karl's books with great frequency and so he began to look for it in the night skies of the spring and summer. And one night, there it was, larger than he imagined while reading any of his books, but unmistakable, and oh, so quiet and grand. Looking up at the majesty of Bootes revealed the constellation to be the most impressive thing he had ever seen. Karl found himself awed with its size and the great sense of serenity the odd constellation seemed to convey. Now, finally, they would meet.

"Karl had dozed, but not for very long. He was awakened by a chime, and the conductor's voice. "On your right, those of you in the odd numbered compartments, is the great constellation Bootes, The Herdsman."

"Karl gazed through the glass into the darkness. The light of the stars was clarity itself. The grandiose, slightly crooked and unique shape of the constellation, something like a huge, elongated, crooked kite, was somehow sad, but noble. There was a lofty stateliness in its shape, even at this proximity. And there was just no mistaking it. The voice seemed directed at Karl.

"Bootes is the Herdsman, the Shepard. My pride is the venerable giant, Arcturus. But Arcturus, the brightest light in the northern sky, that quiet elegance, is my sadness as well. For as this giant, some 20 million miles in diameter with luminosity more than one hundred times that of your own sun, soars through space at 90 miles a second…and will soon be leaving us. Arcturus, my alpha star, is one of the prominent few stars to reside high above our galactic plane. A mere two million years ago Arcturus was some 800 million light years from Earth. Now, he is only 37 light years distant. But soon, as the time for his Milky Way visit draws to a close, Arcturus will leave us in this galaxy forever, bound for regions toward the constellation Vela in your southern hemisphere. We will miss his soft brilliance, his dignity. But for many springs and summers yet to come, if you are lonesome or alone, look up. Gaze upon and enjoy the glow of this guardian of the bear while you may. In half a million years, you shall see his splendor no more. But for now, we wait for you and shall be your companions in the night. And you will never be alone."

"Karl felt sad…but somehow no sadder than when he first beheld Bootes in the summer sky that cool night. Distances seemed to be of little consequence. But now, he knew, he would never feel lonesome or alone again. He had but to seek out Bootes in the quiet darkness of the spring and summer skies. And enjoy the warmth and powerful dignity of Arcturus while he could.

"There was a take-along supper given out to all aboard while the Bullet made its way back to Constellation Station. And as Karl prepared to detrain the conductor approached him with a jolly smile and a book shaped package. He handed it to Karl.

"I'm sorry we couldn't visit that lovely jewel box, the Pleiades, this trip. We were running a bit late, and you know, trains, especially great trains, must never, never be late! Perhaps next time, when we plan to pay a visit to Pegasus, the Flying Horse, as well. But, I do have a memento of this trip for you." The conductor handed Karl the package.

"What is it," asked Karl?

"Why, it's a book of maps," said the conductor. "With careful reading, it can guide you right back here, if you feel sad and miss us. You're never alone with a good book, you know!"

"Karl knew he would be back to see the regal Leo the Lion, Ursa Major the Great Bear, Hercules, and Taurus, the Bull. But for now, he thanked the pot-bellied conductor, who was consulting his watch again, and headed for home. As he walked away from Constellation Station, Karl couldn't help but feel a little sad, but it was a wonderful trip and somehow he knew he would be back.

"In the distance, the soft, warm glow of familiar house lights became visible. It was good to be home after all.

"Karl opened the book of maps. Inside, however, there were no maps. There seemed to be...a story! It began: "Through his room window Karl could see the night was thick but he could see pinpoints of gold and patches of orange light scattered along the horizon. Soon, thought Karl, he would reach Constellation Station....

SPEEDTRAP

Thing is, life on planet Earth got very oppressive, for Harold; for everyone. But Harold, unlike many stranded citizens had the means to escape; the capital and the will. So he sent away to Amazon Steroid for the new do-it-yourself space ship kit, deluxe model, complete with documents and decals and set about putting the thing together in his basement. He packed the trunk with spare clothing and several nutria-systems meals as well as a booklet with the telephone numbers of his two friends and Morris the Seltzer Man's delivery service. Most friends' phones were always busy and unreachable but having their numbers offered a feeling of security. He would have included other emergency numbers in his book but on the entire planet there were no other services or contacts available...or existent.

Of course the ship, on completion, was too unwieldy to remove from his basement, so poor Harold had to contract for the removal of the side of his house first. Inconvenient to be sure, but as he was space bound Harold did not intend on returning and did not mind the destruction, in fact, he watched the operation with a certain glee and delight. Harold's neighbors were understandably disturbed at the unholy mess on his lawn but because of political correctness they smiled and said nothing. The unsightly heap of rubble was nothing on the agitation scale, however, compared to the moment Harold's rocket lifted off. Windows cracked and shattered for blocks, walls buckled, dishes, bottles and crockery vibrated, broke and exploded, houses collapsed and some caught fire. In fact, Harold's front lawn no longer stood out and pretty much looked like everyone else's within a five block radius. Many people were overheard saying: "What happened?" And, as usual, few people knew. Radio and television reception was lost for days. Computer information vaporized.

Harold, meanwhile, was merrily cruising along through outer space, and tuned to his SETI station, hoping he would not run into any close encounters of any kind. But as he was counting his blessings: no more taxes, no more registration forms, no more government, bureau and administration papers, as he was rounding a narrow passage between two innocent looking asteroids on his way to one of Saturn's friendlier satellites, he spotted a strange black and white vehicle with flashing lights gaining on him.

Moments later the craft was flanking his, and he could hear the unwelcome sonorous command: "You… pull over!"

Harold pulled over and the indescribable character inside the craft stepped out of it into space, motioned Harold to roll down his window and said:

"Do you know how fast you were going?"

TIME STUFF

TIME AND TIME AGAIN

I recall that stretch of concrete some 75 yards or so alongside the Westside highway in upper Manhattan, beneath the bland brick apartments overlooking the Hudson. The gaping crevice housed by this concrete block called to mind some kind of dump, an accidental waste disposal of convenience. But deep inside was my modest lab, nothing more than two rooms behind a gray steel portal which was never used. My entry was from one of the freight elevators in the towering apartment building above. A combination of three buttons pressed in sequence took the lift to the subbasement. From there, another steel door; beyond that, the lab...and my...machine.

My partners, Henri Duquesne and Carl Kaiser shared a Pied a Terre in those apartments above, so they had taken only a short time in answering my summons when I called. How clearly, as if it were only moments ago, I recall Henri's first words on his arrival: "Developments? Progress?" he asked with some enthusiasm. Indeed I had a development to report, one that would change everything for each of us, forever. Carl circled my capsule and peered through the Lucite panels.

"I don't remember these," he said. "New?"

"The panels serve as reinforcement to the inside windows we already installed. Let me tell you what we've got."

Carl seated himself on the old recliner I'd purchased nearly a decade ago when the project first began. He opened a package of fresh mints and slipped one on his tongue.

"This is like the opener of H.G. Wells' Time Machine," I began, "when the fundamentals of what we are doing are explained and demonstrated. Well, I won't bore you with the elemental details you are so familiar with, but we have instituted some improvements and hopefully brought, some of what, up until now, has only been theory, to...pardon the pun, light."

In his Special Theory of Relativity published in 1905, Einstein posited that if the speed of light could be exceeded we might possibly overtake that light, bearing our recorded history, and witness our past; just as stars we can see now might no longer exist. It is their light which shows these bodies as they were hundreds, thousands, even millions of years ago. Today only their light might exist, as might *our* light exist to viewers on these stars, showing our planet as it was hundreds, thousands, even millions of years ago!

But the speed of light is no easy barrier to approach, much less overtake. It is no simple designation being merely the speed at which light travels. It is an absolute speed, at which nothing can travel faster. Further, the effects suffered traveling at such overwhelming speeds can be devastating, destructive, odd, bizarre, and worst of all, unexpected...not the least of which is the actual slowing down of one's own, body clock. Time, for the traveler at light speeds, can virtually slow to negligible...if not stop altogether.

The expense, the technical difficulties and the scheduling of a real trip proved themselves to be overwhelming and insurmountable so we have innovatively come upon the odd idea of attempting a simulation of the actual physical time-trip. Duplicating what we have calculated to be the physical effects of traveling at light speeds, we have succeed in creating a durable titanium pod, equipped with devices that will emit the stress, vibration and damage that would be expected and unavoidable if such a physical voyage were to be taking place. Of course, the pod and travelers would also be fit with prophylaxis to prevent, forestall and repair such effects. It is much of this that has taken the better part of the decade.

"Gentlemen," I said, commanding the attention of the small group, "we know we cannot physically undertake our little time-traveling voyage in physical space...but the effects should be the same, that is, we should net the same results, in *time*. Why must we traverse space? What I have now definitely discovered in these many months is that light, past light, present light, future light, all light, travels not only in space, but in *time* as well. And it is *that* light that we shall travel through...and in doing so travel back in time!"

The shell surrounding the pod was fit with light projectors, all synched with motion, vibration and sound; all coordinated with temperature, pressure and g-force activators. We were almost ready for the maiden journey...the mini voyage which would only last no more than a few minutes. I reached into the pod and removed the protective suits I had stored in the unit.

"Behold, your time-travel suits! Attire for the ages! Remember," I directed my comment to Carl, as Henri was still examining the air-tight, studded, triple shielded capsule, "if we have any indication of trouble or sense anything at all going wrong, we can call a halt to this.... We can stop it. Bear in mind we are still on Earth, right here, in this room, in this space! And that, is the beauty of the simulation! Of course," I smiled at my fellow travelers, "if our light simulation links up with our time-line light, what we will be seeing through the glass and Lucite panels will belie that. And hopefully, we will see...something of our yesterdays!"

Henri struggled with his suit and then poured himself something from one of the decanters on a silver tea-cart. Carl asked if he could join him, and poured me one as well.

"To Godspeed," Carl said, raising his glass. And I recall how the three of us savored the drink, although with some angst and trepidation.

Carl was the designated outside monitor for the first try. Then Henri would take his place and Carl and I would make the trip... all of us to compare notes later on that evening. "I'll be dressed when you return," he said. It would only be a few minutes. Carl saluted the capsule.

I recall how Henri carefully stepped on board, mindful of strapping himself into the deep seat.

"I feel a trifle silly," he said.

We hooked the doors securely to the chassis, ran through a brief check, not unlike those run by pilots prior to flight, and, after fastening our suits, threw the appropriate switches. The vibrations thrilled our receptors from head to toe, then the lights began to flash past the panels, revealing at first only bright patches, but then clear images rushing by, accompanied by muffled sounds of farmland, warfare, the river, rising and falling, seasons, snows, ice, foliage, ferns, vines, blurred savages, fires, animals, beasts, more snows, ice. It was all beyond captivating. I don't know how long we stared through the panels, riveted.

I can remember telling Henri that we must have miscalculated setting the duration of our trip. It was only to have been a few moments. And according to his watch, it was. But there was apparently no way we could have reckoned with the overwhelming speed of light. I joked that we might have to live in the past.

I told an ashen Henri not to be concerned. We could reverse the light and travel back. But we were already there: far, far, into the future; the real future. Our clocks, simulation or no, had, indeed, all but stopped. Time for us *had* slowed immeasurably as the world in which we both lived had moved on - perhaps thousands of years.

Henri tried to laugh. "Can you stop the vibration? And the lights! Can you stop the light! All we need to do is un-strap, unhook, and open the pod." I remember how his hands and voice shook as he barely intoned "Thank God we're only in the lab...over the highway."

And we unhooked, unbuckled, and looked through the panels before checking our suits and opening the doors. It was dark. There was no Carl, no lab, no steel paneled door overlooking…anything. There was nothing there. Nothing! Our clocks had slowed, with every simulated vibration, with every accompanying light wave. We had traveled perhaps hundreds of thousands of years into the past as old Carl, our planet, our world, our universe, had moved the equal and opposite hundreds of thousands of years - light years - into the future: a future of darkness. Newton's foreboding words ringing in my mind: 'For every action…an equal and opposite reaction!'

No planets, no stars, no galaxies; the future was…a future of nothingness...of no one; nothing; darkness; no one but poor Henri and me; nothing more. I hoped we might at least have something - to talk about. For a little while.

*

Carl stood by, finishing his drink, then pouring himself another, and became increasingly concerned. It had been more than the few minutes Dr. West and Henri predicted; the vibrations of the pod had ceased; the light seemed to have stabilized; the flickering stopped and an eerie silence prevailed. The pod doors remained closed. There was no movement within. No one emerged.

And as the ashen physicist cautiously approached the stilled, now muted, titanium craft, a double knock on the lab's front door broke the white silence as well as Carl's mesmerized trance. How long had he been standing in his rapt stupor? With a mixture of distraction and relief he opened the door in three quick strides. It could only have been the group's tacit partner, their lookout and "gofer," Werner. It was because of Werner's pet name and his sporadic commitment to the group – he was there…he wasn't there; he shone…he didn't shine…that he was affectionately known as Schrodinger. But Schrodinger was loyal and capable, and physics was his life…when he was available.

Dressed in baggy clothing and jeans he stood smiling in the windy hallway's grey lighting, arms outstretched. "And," he said? His expression changed instantly as he beheld that on Carl's face.

"They were to have returned minutes ago…more…," he said. "There's no sign of them.

"Really," said Schrodinger. "Can I come in?"

"Of course, of course. Sorry. I don't know what to do. We weren't quite prepared for this at all. They were supposed to open the pod doors after only a few moments. The vibrations stopped. The lights are bright. Other than that nothing has changed. But where are they?"

Werner looked over at the time-craft. "And you've been here the whole time," he said?

"Of course."

The recent arrival put a hand on Carl's shoulder. "Let's have a look."

Werner walked over to the pod and peered inside. "There's no one inside," he said. "Are you sure…"

"Of course," said Carl, brushing his face. "I've been here all this while. I was here when they left. It was only to be a few minutes, then I was going to go with West. This was supposed to be the…the maiden voyage. You were going to go after me, if everything worked. I was to go next!" Carl put his hand on his head.

"Are you sure there isn't some remote control somewhere out here…; something perhaps you forgot?"

"No…, of course not."

"Let me have a look inside," said Werner. He stepped over to the pod and lifted the steel bar sitting across the side of the craft, opening the door. "Nothing. It seems as if nothing has been disturbed" He scoured the instrument panel.

Carl said, "they were only gone a very short time.

"It doesn't take much," muttered Schrodinger. "And, in fact, it looks as if they traveled a considerable stretch back in time, according to this dash lever. Look, it's down several millimeters."

Carl poked his head into the mini-cockpit. "It doesn't look like much."

"Again," said Werner, "it doesn't take much. But West knew that. Don't forget, you're traveling at close too light speeds. They probably found themselves captivated by the landscapes…the history…, what they could catch of it. Then, when they tried to come back…they didn't even need to reverse. Their clocks had already slowed. We…and the Earth had moved on…the stars…the galaxies had moved on…as had our time! Hard to say how far into the future they went when they returned…but it's safe to say Dr. West made a miscalculation…. I will say, where <u>they</u> are, we are long gone! But it wasn't West's fault. The experience was overwhelming. They stayed away, according to <u>our</u> clocks, too long…though it seemed to <u>us</u> like moments. According to <u>their</u> clocks it seemed like minutes, but measured by their light speeds and near time-stopping rate, it was eons." Werner took out a slide rule and a mini- calculator from his back pocket. "Let me show you something, Carl." He worked the ruler and held up his calculator. "This is just to check. You won't believe this…. I'm hoping I can reduce the time and distances they traveled….on this pod of course! Perhaps, I can even show you!"

Schrodinger made a few calculations, and then peered onto the pod cockpit. "Just as I thought," he said, "somehow these gradations are far too wide. I think I can…possibly reduce the movements of the levers between spaces substantially. We could send the craft, say, to the 1950's, instead of the beginning of the Common Era, which it seems like West and Duquesne visited. It's chancy, but I cannot believe that a short dash just a few years, which would not take more than a few nanoseconds….would not deliver me… safely… back here. My computer says it would…the calculations at these speeds are not putting me any deeper in the future than…here! It's a risk …but I'm more than willing. Perhaps…I might even stumble on those two. What say, Carl?"

It was more than apparent, but Carl was still in a strange state. Call it shock, disbelief, certain numbness. Schrodinger, despite his mathematical prowess, had no such connection to reality, or, to make things easier for him, any cares, social connections or mundane responsibilities beyond his loves of theoretical physics and Dr. West's little group. Carl, none of his color having returned, was non-committal.

"I'm going to do it Carl! The craft seems in excellent shape…not a dent, hardly a smudge. You don't need to come, Carl. But, for me, nothing ventured, nothing gained. I know I'll be alright! We'll be back with you in mere moments. I promise! Prepare to write it up. We'll be famous! And why don't you send out for something to eat while you're waiting! I'm hungry already!"

With that Werner hunched down to get into the pod that he had helped build, ran though the check list he and Dr. West had devised, saluted Carl and shut the pod door.

In a way, it is unfortunate to report that although poor Schrodinger's mathematical calculations were indeed correct, and his physical adjustments to the pod's dashboard were exacting and delicate enough, and the spacing between millimeters were microscopically fine tuned, his numbers were not wrong…and he did land in the fifties…and he would have been back in seconds…the ratios were correct…but he was stuck! The overheated levers were melted and out of whack, on the fritz and kaput!

The fifties window might have been closed for some, but it was now wide open for Werner; he was stuck here, and he'd have to walk back. He'd make it back to Carl and to the lab in the promised few moments, but it would be a long walk back, and it would take him about fifty years!

Schrödinger got out of his busted cockpit looked around at a repaved Westside Highway, the single level George Washington Bridge, and the bright colored automobiles. Things didn't look too different…and they didn't look so bad.

*

Moments later Carl turned around to answer yet another knock on the lab door. Strange, a tired looking eighty year old man stood at the door. Of course he bore a distinct resemblance to Schrodinger athough it didn't seem plausible that the trip could have aged him all *that* much.

"Sorry," said Werner, I knew I'd get back here in time; I just didn't think it would take fifty years! Did you get the food? Let's eat!

NOTE

There are rainy days when one contemplates some rather esoteric notions...and this was one of them, a stubborn notion which seemed steeped in inexplicable paradox, and which refused to yield anything approximating resolution...nor even a hint at clarification.

Beyond the complex exercise of determining who one essentially is, where one essentially comes from and where, after this current adventure one is headed, were the added question and the seeming impossible difficulty of obtaining substantive proof. It was the added singular riddle of how to establish tangible evidence of his theory; validation that one actually existed at a prior time, and further, some kind of attesting connection was sought that, after "passage", one would eventually reappear here once again!

His good friend Marlow would have been an excellent conversational confederate. He was bright, thoughtful, and as philosophically capable as anyone to probe his friend's notions but he was adamant about partaking in any religious or political discussions. And the past identities, resurrections, futures and destinies of one's consciousness were too close to religion for Marlow to give any sincere thought or serious discourse to.

Merely embarking upon the the subject of a validating proof or the possibility of a connecting thread between times and existence would require delving into the very core of one's consciousness and identity, if the word "identity" is applicable. It is the key to one's being that was sought. "Identity" might serve to distract and confuse. What is the true nature of one's consciousness? What could comprise a true "identity"? Time and place were only backgrounds, and inconsequential.

Lest the subject be alien and strange to the reader, one needs to understand that the elements contributing to, and creating, identity are lost in, let us say, transit. Physical and mental traits and abilities are gone from the equation along with memory.

To speculate that the consciousness will be able to look "back" or remember is easily squashed by being clearly aware as to how opaque is the recollection of any past life. Memory of the past is gone as is any physical connection to the future.

Thus we have the conundrum of: the **past self** leaving substantiating word intended for the **future self,** or (to clarify this difficulty) the **current self** leaving some kind of evidence to be found by the **future self!** How could either of the "selves" (past or current) communicate or leave word for their "extensions"... if no immutable or enduring knowledge of the future exists for them?

The question was put to Marlow. Where...would "word" be placed (by the current self) to insure its discovery...by the "future self"? How could notification be affected? What thread could initiate an alarm and convey a genuine connection? Essentially this was communication from one time to another! Was it possible? Shadowy consolation was lurking, ghosting in the existence of the remnants of history, chronicles...relics, artifacts! It seemed a paradox. And, indeed, Marlow gave the question little thought when he quickly confessed "no answer." Somehow, however inexplicably, the question nagged and persisted.

Ruminating on the problem gave rise to its counterpart paradox: Where would past self place a communication, evidence, a note... that would assure receipt by future self...(actually current self)? Again the question was put to Marlow to no avail. (Although it was he who affably gifted faint and subtle reminders of the question: one of which was an ancient padlock, with no key.)

Frequently considered were places one had been to...some time and again. Were there favorites? Places sure to repeatedly beckon which had harbored secret recesses known to...? Were there nooks, niches favored only by...? If there were, how would one convey such a place to a singular self not yet extant? Marlow's lock chidingly sat on a shelf between books.

Could books be a consideration? An ancient volume having journeyed through time; classic epics whose pages had long yellowed and begun to flake; a leather bound family Bible...? He began to probe books. Stories, science, psychology, Freud, Adler, Jung; philosophy, Hegel, Locke, Kant Hume; collectibles, travel, politics, mathematics, history, reference, humor, favorites, mystery, intrigue, espionage, war, science fiction, childhood, keepsakes. There were collections; early Modern Library editions, school texts. How many were travelers from another generation? How many would survive beyond this generation? Would an entry to a distant tomorrow survive? Where...and in whose keeping? A folded paper, a note? Where?... Discovered...where? and by whom? There could only be by the intended.

And then it occurred to him! Where would *his* former self have placed *his* alarm?; *his* communication?

This, if there were any hope of his leaving a message would serve as a track, a pathway to follow. And, there need not be any diversity. They, the senders, would, of course, be one and the same...in thought, in intention, in discovery! That is, if there were any comparable character and quality to his theory of his "eternal" traveling consciousness! Otherwise, he thought encouragingly, none of this, none of his efforts, none of his thought, would make any sense. And he knew, somehow he deeply believed, that was not possible. Otherwise, nothing made sense to him.

*

Since one of his bookshelves had recently collapsed, virtually exploding under the burden of far too heavy a load, for far too long a time, a new and interesting unit was on its way after several weeks of intense searching. Only it was not "new", it was a rather ornate, interesting, and quite substantial antique piece. Further, however, adding to its character, if not somehow taking away from its antiquity, if not its value, was a bar compartment that he had his heart set on, and had gone through the time and considerable expense of installing. The new addition was unobtrusive and smoothly blended into the shape, design and apparent age of the older nearly floor to ceiling bookcase.

The only difficulty posed by the new bar, and its additional glass shelf, was accommodating its elaborate mirrored back panel, lit by an overhead fluorescent light. The light's long cord, of course, required access to the wall outlet behind the bookcase, all of which was doubly paneled and not particularly accommodating as a conduit for wiring...or anything!

It may only have been a few weeks; likely was more, but it was enough time to illustrate how daunting a task it was to find his Holy Grail within any of the thousands of pages already well perused. The chore, perhaps at Marlow's genially rebuking "I told you so", was abandoned.

It was on that very late afternoon as consolation was sought following some mechanical rearrangement of books, that the bar was opened, two of its drinks set standing on the open shelf, reflecting their images and the compartment's fluorescent's light from the shelf above in the mirror, when the light went out.

It should've been uneventful to reach through the opening in the bookcase's bottom drawer, gaining access to the wall outlet but, of course the opening was not exactly aligned with the socket...nor, now, with the ejected chord, which because of its being somewhat truncated found itself out of the wall unit...although with some miraculous manipulation it could be reinserted.

As he stuck his hand through the drawer and the back panel's opening to reach the disconnected plug he noticed that there were really two panels forming the one covering panel... which was prematurely coming apart. And through the opening he could see the corner of a piece of paper probably large enough to write a note on. He reconnected the errant cord and stood to find something thin enough to fit through the narrow crack between the panels to allow extricating the yellowed paper.

What he hastily found was a similar piece of paper with which, if careful, he could possibly capture the one visible rough edge of what he could see and draw the thing out.

As a lark he quickly scribbled a silly note and fastened a protruding piece of tape to one end which he gently inserted into the opening between the panels telling himself that he might oddly have possibly discovered his message venue.

Carefully and slowly putting his arm through the bookcase bottom drawer once again he inserted his paper through the opening, tape first barely contacting the other paper. But in trying to cause some adhesion to the tape he had to relinquish his already insecure two finger grip. As he pressed his "extractor" a millimeter forward he could feel his weak grip loosen. Between his two fingers he now tenuously held both pieces, the difference between them discernible only by a slight difference in shade. In trying, finally, to somehow obtain better contact, with the paper he was attempting to grasp, he made one last effort to advance his grip, noticing as he did so, he could barely tell which slip of paper was which. And then, one of the two pieces slipped away and down through the crack.

The thing was gone, as he held on to what he thought was his piece. But there was no tape protruding from the edge and nothing sticky to the touch where he had attached the adhesive.

His glance fell on his note. On it was almost exactly what he had written but it was in pencil and faded. He studied the message and now knew exactly where to deposit it, knowing it will eventually be well received.

With the fluorescent light reconnected and the mirror's reflection brightening the new bar, his drinks stood chilled and ready. Cheers!

THE RETURN

In my pocket I have a Saint Gaudens twenty-dollar gold piece with the date worn to obscurity. For some, this will assuredly not suffice as any kind of proof of this story, although perhaps inherent reason and logic will furnish adequate confirmation of what took place.

The house could have been any Washington Heights apartment building. But to me it was mine; where I had always lived. The color of its brick was off-white. It stood on the corner of 178th Street and Cabrini Boulevard on the upper Westside of Manhattan, across the street from the immense George Washington Bridge which spanned the Hudson to Fort Lee, New Jersey.

On hot summer evenings we would bring folding chairs downstairs to the corner and sit up late into the night with neighbors, enjoying the breeze from the river, keeping cool.

Old Mr. Collins, who had been building superintendent at one time, was almost always there. A big man, and former U.S. Marine who had fought in the Spanish-American War, he was a retired mounted policeman and one time keeper of the small red lighthouse, situated on the rocks of the Hudson beneath the bridge. Mr. Collins was the nucleus of the group and I felt a special importance because he lived on our floor, around the bend in apartment 4A.

Mrs. Berman, from upstairs on the 5th floor, was almost always in attendance as well. She was getting very old and quiet and I cannot recall anything to characterize her beyond: Mrs. Berman, 5th floor, upstairs.

There were also the Millers and the Schweds, ground floor neighbors who were best friends and whose children enjoyed the additional convenience of receiving ice-cream money or jackets through windows without having to go inside.

Others passed by and stopped to talk but were by no means regulars. They were only, not unfamiliar, faces. Neighbors who never sat down, outside on the corner, with us those hot summer nights.

I had spent many a summer vacation away. How odd the six-story house seemed when I returned. It was not strange, because it was so familiar. It was not different. It had not changed at all. It was odd, because I had changed and it had not. It occurred to me that I had moved, been away and grown while the house had not. It was, during those late, hot, dry summer days, as always, tall and quiet, on the corner, off white. Each window was familiar, as was each pavement crack, and scratched and painted initials on the bricks, chinks and notched crevices in the cement between. They were all still there, as I had left them. Nothing had changed. Yet.

In time, a long expressway would be built; some blocks east, a bus terminal. And the house on Cabrini Boulevard was razed. Only memories were left of its cool image in the early evening blue, waiting as we came back from Broadway, the taste of a chocolate soda still on our lips. Hours later, its early morning smile would reflect the sun's glare. But now its familiar, informal reign on the windy corner for 25 years was over.

I had been away and alone and had on occasion been obsessed with thoughts of the old neighborhood, particularly the house. I pictured the corner, the street and the sidewalk in front of the building. During one of these mental excursions I focused on an almost forgotten detail.

In front of the apartment house, built into the sidewalk, was a black, iron trap door. It opened on a coal chute to the cellar and was used exclusively for the delivery of coal. The major difference between this and other neighborhood coal chutes was it was on the sidewalk, not vertically built into the side of the building. It was smaller than the iron doors found on street freight elevators and could be opened with a single finger or crowbar inserted into a hole across from the hinge. The door was about two feet square.

Shortly after the new expressway was completed I had been back to the old street and found in place of our house, a pleasant bit of park, raised and set back several feet. Around and above the little park area ran the expressway. Otherwise, except for a breezy emptiness, everything was the same. I had not noticed anything more.

I came to wonder if they hadn't done away with the iron door. Most likely they had, although I did not recall any apparent change in the pavement and why alter the street since the little park was built a considerable distance back from it? It was then I became preoccupied with thoughts of the coal chute and thought, if it was still there where did it now lead? I had seen where many times as a child.

It was on a vacant day in September, I decided, out of a peculiar mixture of nostalgia and curiosity, to revisit the site of my old beloved house. It was a long walk from the Fort Washington Avenue bus stop, made even longer by the emptiness in the streets, the lack of familiar faces; the bowing warp of time. The walls of the buildings still standing, the familiar landmarks, seemed mute with the shyness of a child who has not seen a friend in a long time. The warmth in the air waited to be shook by the shrill call of one boy to another or the whipping swing of a stick-ball bat putting a pink ball high on a flower-potted fire escape, or the song of the huckster selling fruit, cashing clothes or sharpening knives.

Looking up I could see the apartment where Ross used to live. Behind it, I thought I saw Ross and his mother and father, his big brother Irv, and myself, sitting in the living room waiting to go downstairs. On my left was Bernie's window. There was no shade, no curtain hanging. I knocked. It was dusty and black on the inside. I waited. No one came.

The house was only a half block away. On the corner was Biderman's grocery store. I could see it was closed but I quickened my pace, nearly breaking into a jog, because in Biderman's you could get salami on a hard roll, ice cold Doc's Root Beer and fresh chocolate or vanilla frosted cupcakes from the box. Jack the postman was often inside eating lunch, sitting on the one wooden and wrought iron stool that stood forever before Biderman's marble topped counter. Lenny the salesman, stopping in on his way home, would tell a funny story while buying groceries, and Harry, Biderman's assistant, pencil behind his ear, leaning on the counter top was, on slow afternoons, good for a coin trick, catching flies, or moving his ears. To his left were neatly placed boxes of Joyva Halvah, chocolate-covered jellies and marshmallow twists for two cents apiece. I stood before the mini-flight of three concrete steps leaning into the store. Years ago, when Biderman's was in its heyday, and nearly everyone in the neighborhood shopped there to some degree, I overheard someone say it was a goldmine. Since Biderman's son didn't want any part of the place and Biderman was aging, some people jealously remarked about Harry's good fortune as heir apparent to the place. After all, he wasn't even a relation; just a hired young man. Now, some hardware and a couple of pairs of workman's gloves hung on the door-window.

Across the street were the park, the emptiness and, not seeming strange at all, just where it had always been, the iron door. I stopped in front of it, and through the rainbow emanating from the park, paused to dream of slug, bike rides, scooters and skates and the grinding racket their wheels made on the concrete sidewalk And I could envision a little boy standing on that very spot. For a moment I thought of going home, but the notion gave way to scanning the area. Was I being observed? It was then I reached down, as if to tie my shoelace, and inserted a finger through the hole opposite the rusting hinge. The door was heavy but opened easily as if it were not I who was lifting it but the winds of the past blowing it open for me.

The opening disclosed a gaping blackness. Of course, I expected nothing more. Sitting on the edge, my legs dangling in the hole, I took hold of one side and swung down into the pit, none too deftly, landing on a heap of coal. The shock of falling made me stop moving for a moment. Time itself seemed to have come to an abrupt halt. Then, as I attempted to step down, the coal gave way and I fell backward. Objects in the room began to swirl gently as they came into focus and took strange shapes. It was as if time and space were moving together, backward and away. It was not unlike eyes getting used to the dark.

When I got to my feet and stumbled down off the coal heap I could make out the room. The contour of its dimensions was vividly familiar. It was the last of a chain of rooms and storage closets in the cellar of the old house. Were the others still in tact as well? I could make out a door ahead. Certainly, I reasoned, the door led somewhere. It was splintered, dusty and forbidding, but it had another side. As I reached for it, I realized the knob was gone but I managed to get the door open, like the sidewalk door, with a finger. One room led to the next. And not unexpectedly, they were all there: the carriage room, the boiler room, the storage room, the laundry room, the workshop, the incinerator and then, finally, incredibly, the elevator.

A rush of memories returned to me: Willie the handyman taking what seemed like weeks to paint my little red car white; Henry the elevator man bringing the car up to the apartment, where I then quickly outgrew it and it was relegated to becoming a receptacle for newspapers and magazines. I saw myself watching the final cycle of a washing machine, helping my mother hang clothes, and years later, exploring the dark basement labyrinths with a friend after school…with the aid of matchbooks. The explorations had become less exciting when we began using what we thought would be the more efficient candles. Nothing could equal the pressure and urgency, the chill of the blackness and nebulous danger when the match burned down and out. And nothing was as inevitable as the brief life span of the paper match, hardly equal to the two elements in our explorations that always loomed before us. Always presenting hidden danger, always possibilities that could frighten us to death, always lurking were: the superintendent…and the dog. We bravely stood ready to deal with them but our progress, that is, the high tech move to candles, and later to flashlights, not only lessened the surprise of these dangers and softened the challenges of our underground explorations, they dampened the entire experience, and soon put an end to them as well.

As I rang for the elevator I watched the red arrow, which pointed down, begin to glow. Through the round glass window in the door I could see the cables move and faintly was able to hear a hum from within the elevator shaft. Other than that persistent sound everything remained probably as still as it had been for the past two decades. I had to wonder where the elevator was coming from. I knew there was no house. The building had been taken down years ago. Yet I was following what seemed to be a logical sequence of events. Was this making sense? The hum stopped and the inner elevator door opened.

I pulled at the outer door and stepping in recognized the peculiar designs on the walls. There were old scratched and worn black buttons. Everything was exactly as I recalled and the words, "coincidence," "nightmare," and "hallucination," came to mind. I wiped perspiration from my face, my legs felt weak and shaky; my body began to shiver involuntarily. And already, without being aware of it, the thought had crossed my mind, terrifying me. There was one supreme test, one inevitability, one place to go. With some reservation, but yet determined, I pressed the fourth floor button.

As I ascended, the light which came through the little chicken wire round hole became brighter with each floor. The car came to a stop at four, the inner door opened, and I pushed at the heavier door to step off.

Across from the elevator was a large hall window. Outside, below, was the courtyard littered with glass, paper and small planks of wood.

It was a treasure trove for young pirates, who would, despite informal prohibitions, be sure to climb daily through the ground floor access windows to sift through the debris. Sun suffused the six stories above the yard, shining on the refuse with gleams, increasing its apparent value to the impish hunters a thousand fold.

I crossed the floor parallel with the stairwell to the first apartment on the left of the elevator, 4E, my old apartment. For a moment I stood before it. Everything was, or seemed, as it had always been: the brown door flecked with gold paint, the fading welcome mat, the protruding bell, the only one on the floor which had not been painted over, our name beneath it. I distracted myself with thoughts of the Collins' around the bend in 4A, the Millers downstairs, and Mrs. Berman above, on 5. So far, however, I reminded myself, I had not seen a soul. Numb, I stood transfixed. Then I pressed the bell. I remembered the ring.

"Who is it" a small but pleasant sounding voice asked from behind the door. I hesitated.

"A…visitor," I replied. And at once I had a startling recollection. I had experienced a similar incident when I was a boy. Someone had rung the bell and when I inquired as to who it was the voice responded with, "a visitor." Although I had repeatedly been instructed never to open the door to strangers, I recall having had a contrary compulsion to do so. It was almost as if I had known my own father was there. The door opened wide.

Speech seemed to catch in my throat.

"Hello," I managed. The boy was me as a child, about eight or nine years old. I couldn't take my eyes from him. I wanted to grab him up and take him with me, show him everything I knew and teach him a thousand things. I felt compelled to give him countless warnings. I wanted to bestow on him all my possessions. Beyond the boy I could see past his yellow slip-over sweater, through the little foyer and into the living room along the furniture I knew so well. Each piece was in its proper place. I wanted to touch every article; sit at the table; turn on the lamp; feel the chairs again. Instead, I could only stand, immobile, in my place.

"My mother isn't home," the little boy said, his eyes clear and blue. For an instant I saw myself staring out into an adult world of truths and perplexities however modified by my own childish concepts and feelings. I had the feeling of understanding him completely.

"Well…," I said softly, "it doesn't really matter. I have something I want to give to you."

In my pocket, I always carried a gold coin which was given to me when I was a young boy by the stranger whom I found standing at my door that afternoon. He had paid his visit for no other apparent reason. I remember being struck by the word "Liberty" engraved on the coin…and its being solid gold.

"Keep this and don't lose it," I said. "And don't let anyone take it away from you." He took it and fondled it.

"Thanks," he drew out as he admired it. "Can I really keep it?"

"It's yours," I said. "Perhaps I'll see you again."

Then I left. The elevator was waiting. I pressed "B" and took it to the basement; I ran through the cellar rooms to the coal bin, climbed through the iron door and pulled myself up into the street. On my way to the Fort Washington Avenue bus stop I turned around but once, only to see the blowing leaves in the park on Cabrini Boulevard.

Some years had passed. The memory of the coin faded, almost as if I never really owned it. The trip to Cabrini Boulevard could have been a dream. I never went back. The days were fraught with depression and loneliness, at times, an empty coolness draining warmth and life from the body.

It was at the end of a day, on an evening particularly laden with chill, that I answered a knock at my door. I had, for sometime now, been residing in another city, far away, and kept to myself. So when the elderly gentleman at the door, whom I had never set eyes upon before, addressed me by my first name, it was not without surprise.

"I think," he said, "you must know who I am. Or you will." A kindly smile pushed his age aside.

"I'm sorry. I don't believe I do," I replied. "Can I help you?" The old man kept his eyes focused on me as he spoke but seemed to take the opportunity of my reply to peer beyond me and into the apartment.

"I used to live here myself," he paused. "I find myself missing those days quite a bit now."

Smiling, I said, "You couldn't have lived here, this building is brand new."

"Is it?" said the old man. I suddenly realized who he was. He knew I had and he grinned again.

"How is it there?" I gulped out, hardly able to manage clear speech.

"It's the same," he said, "a little lonely."

I was seized with an energy I could not contain. Questions I could not frame as I sensed a certain urgency about him. "Could I go back with you?" He looked about with venerable eyes and said:

"Yes…and no."

"What do you mean," I asked, my heart pounding?

"You cannot go back with me," he said, "but you will go there. Alone."

There was very little light left in the hallway. It had all drained away through cracks and nooks, doors and windows. The old man stood on his side of the threshold in his overcoat, I, on my side, in my shirtsleeves. Behind me, the apartment, darkening, gaping, empty. He put his hand into a deep pocket.

"Incidentally," he said, "I came back here to return this to you. I believe you left it somewhere along the way." He held out the gold piece. It was the St. Gaudens with the date worn away.

"Where did you get it?" I asked.

"An old man gave it to me nearly 35 years ago. You know it's yours."

I looked at the coin's face. The word "Liberty" on it had hardly worn. It was exactly as I had remembered it.

"Keep it and don't lose it," the old man cautioned. He grinned, took a last look beyond me and then disappeared across the hall.

"Will I see you again?" I called after him. He didn't answer. "I'll see you again," I muttered under my breath. But he was gone. Fingering the coin I stepped back into the apartment and closed the door.

Through the open window I could discern the orange image of the faceless sun floating above everything. The air was still but once in awhile some refreshing breeze filled the room.

A QUESTION OF TIME

It seems dining out anywhere without hearing a candled cupcake-bearing coterie singing a lackluster and de-spirited chorus of Happy Birthday is becoming increasingly rare. The fact that most people eventually have a birthday at least every year seems not, however, to have detracted from this most un- extraordinary event in the minds of the celebrants. It is with this phenomenal business in mind that I would like to pose an interesting, if not deflating, question to people of all ages. Call it a kind of hypothetical mind experiment.

Imagine a series of sunspots...or violent storms on the sun, affecting the rotation of the earth on its axis, and the earth is sped up, completing a turn, not in 24 hours, but in something like 12 hours. At the end of several days of this (or weeks or months) would you be older...younger, or the same age had the planet taken 24 hours per turn? Remember, you've now gone through TWICE as many "days" as in former times.

Similarly, suppose the earth slowed down and you go through FEWER "days" (and years) as you would have normally? Suppose rotation stopped altogether? Would you emerge as younger? Would you still age? At the same rate?

Suppose the disturbance on the sun caused the planet to slow in its annual voyage around the sun and caused earth to take some 900 days to make a full journey rather than the usual 365? Are you then YOUNGER? Older? Do you ADD years to your "age"? Are you the same as you WOULD have been during the same "time" period? Or, suppose the trip was expedited and took only 100 days? Would you be adding some three times as many "years" to your age at the end of that period? The new trip could be "accomplishing" that many more "years"...in that "time" period.

And, if the planet stopped altogether? Could you add any days (if rotation ceased)...or years (if revolution stopped) to your life? How could you measure this? According to WHAT? Clocks or calendars become...meaningless!

What I think I seem to be "getting at" here is that TIME would appear to stand alone. Or is it - as Mr. Einstein would have it - "relative?" Or is TIME...TIME?! Mr. Einstein posed that as YOU speed up...your clock slows.

And perhaps as YOU slow down (as is my case) your clock speeds up. And, believe it or not, this HAS been proven. (Although the choral rendition of Happy Birthday seems to go on longer than it takes the coffee to cool.)

Now consider this: light takes some 4.4 years to reach the star Alpha Centauri. A spaceman, could also do it...traveling at that speed; but on return to earth he would find everything gone because many, many MORE years had passed than the mere 8.8 years that it took for the spaceman's round trip. Why is this? Because, according to Einstein,

the spaceman's clock, at the speed of light, slows down. It is NOT ONLY some illusion or physical manifestation. The real clock, the body clock, the ship's clock, the clock measuring TIME, real TIME, slows down. Millions of hours pass on earth during the spaceman's 8.8 years....He has hardly aged, but everyone else on the planet earth is long gone. Many birthdays have passed.

Light travels at some 186,000 miles per second. There are approximately six trillion miles in one light year (the distance light could travel in one year at 186,000 miles per second!) So...find out how many hours are in a year.... At, say, 100 miles per hour, figure how many hours you'd need to go, non-stop, to hit six trillion miles! Or...determine how many hundreds there are in a trillion! This is how many hours you would need to travel when you also multiply this by six (one light year) and then by 4.4 (the distance to Alpha Centauri). This is how long it would take you, traveling at 100 miles an hour, to get there! Too late for lunch, I'm afraid.

And you'd be old! Boy, would you ever be old! And...so would those waiters and waitresses! Don't even ask about the cupcakes!

BTW, for those of you planning on the voyage to Alpha Centauri, several readers were prematurely stopped by the initial "puzzle" of determining how many hundreds there are in a TRILLION. (Alpha C. is 4.4 x Six Trillion miles from us.) Did you do it? (If the answer were, say 2 hundreds, than the star would only be TWO HUNDRED miles away (and two HOURS away) (but of course, that's silly. It is 6x4.4 Trillion! miles away!). So you must find the number of HUNDREDS in a TRILLION. In other words, you must DIVIDE one hundred into one TRILLION. This, of course, is simply done by removing the last two zeros in a TRILLION. We are left with (Voila!) 10,000,000,000! So THIS is the number of HOURS (at 100 mph) it would take you to get there! (If you wish to translate this into days...just, of course, divide again...this time by 24!) Bon voyage!

INFINITE PROBABILITY

UNFINISHED MONKEY BUSINESS

GAF;LK SFDL Q[BMSDF. SKITL DIP DOP.Vksbrug veeksburp pippop nipnap slp slop klincksnain klinksnoon nib inb gib gibn gibris blip giberis…gibberish.

For the most part, that should have been the way the monkeys workel…ah…worked. But it wasn't always so. According to the story "Inflexible Logic" by Russell Maloney (New Yorker Magazine, 1940) reprinted in Clifton Fadiman's entertaining anthology "Fantasia Mathematica" the half dozen (not infinite number) monkeys, although given infinity to accomplish their feat, went ahead, and, pounding the keyboard at random, (as the average primate would be prone to do) typed out, perfectly, many of the world's great works…at the outset of their task!

The expectation had been that, given infinity, the monkeys would strike all the possible letter and word combinations…eventually. But, that should have taken some time. The experimenters were not unprepared to go through reams of nonsense before encountering even a semblance to a reasonable series of words, not to say a complete sentence. What did in fact occur in Mr. Maloney's account, however, was something altogether different, though not contrary to strict logic. The sensible letter combinations, the perfect word constructions simply were struck before the imperfect, nonsensical ones.

In view of the fact that the entire exercise was based on random pounding and not learning experience of any kind, the reversal of expectations is no less probable or logical than thinking the monkeys could produce, or reproduce, a great work after billions of years! A coin flipped enough times will eventually fall on its side…but the odds of its doing so are the same for each flip. The coin might fall on its side on the fiftieth or the first flip. The odds are the same, however great. And, should the coin fall on its side the first flip, the odds of the coin falling on its side the second flip are not increased. The slate is wiped clean. It could fall on its side again! Odds won't change simply because of what just happened.

In Maloney's story a frustrated and confounded mathematician shoots the prolific monkey before he can continue producing classic after infallible classic. I propose this is not really what transpired .The true account of just what occurred has been kept from the public record long enough!

***

Chimpanzee F, Dinty, did manage to finish Uncle Tom's Cabin by Harriet Beecher Stowe, as did his fellow typists in time (with the help of their extensive line of progeny who took up the job when their elders were too old and exhausted) finish all the great and not so great works of literature. These facts were kept secret partially because of the incredulous nature of the public and indeed the incredible nature of the material concerned. Of course, an additional factor may have included the somewhat unscientific and rather whimsical hypothesis upon which the entire business was conducted. The most critical basis, however, for withholding the experiment's results lay in the shocking series of events which developed as time passed…as the chimpanzees continued in their feverish work.

It does seem pointless to speculate; still, it may have been a strange genetic propensity the younger chimps inherited from their parents; perhaps a metaphysical perception capable of closing out the real world (or this one, anyway) of random occurrences. It might have been that without knowing why, (based on pragmatic experience and information) the primates were able, by some unknown system of guidance, always and without fail, to make correct decisions; not unlike some foolish and carefree people who are undeniably, continually, what we call "lucky."

For no apparent reason, they are perpetually at the right places and the right times, and through no homework of their own always seem to make the appropriate times and places...the right moves. These people invariably show up, just in time to catch what turns out to be an uncrowded flight without at all having checked schedules beforehand. It never rains on their vacations. They wander, naively, into the finest restaurants and hotels without having extended the least effort at research or query. Whatever guides them through their infallible, although apparently random, meandering, we call "luck!" Could that same guidance, in stronger concentration, have been responsible for what the monkeys were performing?

Whatever may have been responsible, the monkey's accomplishments surpassed all expectations. After their having typed out all the great works which had already been written, they proceeded to write the great works which had not yet been written. At first, understandably, we had some difficulty discerning exactly what was happening. Our literary team no longer recognized the manuscript pages turned out by the chimps but could see they did not comprise gibberish by any means. It became evident, after extensive research, the little devils had exhausted all of the great letter and word combinations which had at one time or another been set down on paper by the masters. They were now producing the remaining combinations...yet to be created!

The books were marvelous. It was easy to see they were all destined to become future sensations. Neither was it long before our convictions were borne out. Not one week after Ezra (Dinty's son) had completed his first in this new series of yet to be written classics, did the volume receive its rave notice on the front page of the New York Times Book Review. The author was a Russian who had been working on the epic for months. Naturally, he had had no communication with the monkey, and Ezra certainly knew nothing of the Russian (short of writing the man's book!)

Lord knows how we might have capitalized on this turn of events, but as scientists, dedicated only to purposes of our own, however abstract and pointless, the information now at our disposal was put to no bad or dubious use. The new manuscripts were simply catalogued and filed away with the older ones. Yesterday's events, however, may have to change all of that.

Since the original group of simians had completed the written great works, many years had passed. As the newer crews fervently pressed on with their continuing task, the chimps ate, slept, took in a fair share of frolic and also multiplied. The ensuing generations assumed their turns at the typewriters (now computer keyboards), where their ancestors had left off, and manuscripts filled our files and rooms. Not too many more years passed.

Yesterday Ezra's daughter Lena had just finished a most beautiful novel, which, I must confess, we had not read in its entirety, when she inserted a new page into the typewriter she preferred using. No sooner did she underscore the new title and write a half dozen lines, she stopped in the midst of a sentence. She removed the paper, laid it aside, inserted a fresh page, and began yet an entirely new piece.

The monitor, without waiting to see what was to follow, sought me out to report the incident just as he had witnessed it. I rushed to the scene, understandably disturbed, thinking it was finally over. The miracle had apparently, at long last, run its odd course. But this was not so!

One glance over her shoulder and I could see what Lena was now writing was making perfect sense. Yet...how to account for the one discarded page? I lifted it from where Lena had placed it and all became terrifyingly clear. The discarded page read: CHRONICLE OF THE PLANET'S LAST DAYS. There was no author. It went on: "There will doubtless be a shortage of time today, certainly tomorrow, to tell all. Still, an attempt must be made to record at least these last hours here. The chaos and devastation we have all brought down on ourselves for the past several days, ironically, six, may well culminate so we shall all rest on the seventh. As I set this down I have just witnessed a blinding flash to the east…and another to the nor…"

There it finished. Lena had pulled the page from her machine and had placed it atop the pile of already finished manuscripts. The words were apparently to be the last ever written on Earth. But now, the completion of the circle which was to comprise our creations was just beginning. The monkeys, you see, had already typed all those great works WRITTEN, and those that have yet TO BE WRITTEN. Now, Lena had before her, page one of all the great works which will, alas, NEVER BE WRITTEN.

I looked, once more, over the chimpanzee's stooped shoulder. She had already begun typing the book's title: PLANET OF PEACE.

PHASE Nth

There are a number of *keys* to the question of our next destination...if one exists? The nature of these *keys* themselves is cryptic, the *essence* of their components, virtually unknown, their characters alluded to and treated only superficially.

The "keys" to be considered are life; consciousness; memory; time; space...and probability! Let us first check and perhaps clarify, if possible, these factors before addressing the major point:

Life is recognizable by independent movement, growth, reproduction and metabolism, and is often defined by also contrasting it to its opposites...such as inert, dead, insensitive, non-functioning, unresponsive and, of course, un-alive, which, like any list of opposites tells us nothing in a quest for the *essence* of *life* beyond its ostensible definitions.

What we seek is essence, components, what forms the basic, singular, character of life...which distinguishes it from that which is not living - not simply descriptions of its apparent characteristics. We have come as far as DNA and RNA, but their *essence*, the basic component, the primary constituent of *life* remains a mystery. This is not carbon or amino acid!

One feature of *life* is *metabolism* which can be defined as the sum of chemical reactions that take place within the cell of a living organism, providing energy to perform activity and to synthesize new organic material. This important *activity* comprises growth, development and reproduction.

(Organic is that which relates to, or contains, carbon compounds.)

Are we close to defining the essence of *life*? Close,but not at the very basic, mysterious, core. What we can speculate on is the fact that life, so far, cannot be created, and according to a physical principle, might not be quite completely destructible. One stage of life may be temporal but may: have, give rise to, or continue, as subsequent stages...even forms.

What we want to approach is the essence of *consciousness*, which depends on life, although life can stand apart from, at least *higher,* consciousness. So, how to define consciousness, awareness? The philosopher John Locke defined *consciousness* as the perception of what passes through one's mind. And this is partially contingent on sensation emanating from the outside, and the subjective interpretation and formation of those sensations resulting in the final perceptions. Keep in mind that pain, even pleasure, need not be perceived through the medium of language. Infants can experience either (pain or pleasure) prior to any facility with, or even comprehension of, language. Even for an adult the perception of a fragrance or an unpleasant sensation can be experienced superseding any verbal expression!

And, indeed, most sensations and experiences are first perceived prior to their interpretation by, and to, language. But, how...do the initial perceptions come about? How does the knowledge of one's perceiving come about? And how does the memory of those perceptions come about?

It is your awareness of your experiencing, (your undergoing) those sensations. It is your knowledge of this awareness that is consciousness! But what is it that fuels this *awareness*...what brings it to life - consciousness - and what differentiates it from a simple storage bin of sensations? It is as if sensations are compiled in a closed volume,(knowledge) and then the volume is opened and the sensations come to life!... And finally the sensations are conveyed to the individual...by however means...with the final result being consciousness!

It is the depth of this knowledge and the variety (of sensations, experiences) from which it draws that can be characterized by intellect...but that is not at the basis of *consciousness.*

The salient query which might arise here is: How, by what *mechanism*, are these perceptions...this awareness of outside stimulus perceived, even if not communicated? What are its chemical and physical components...and by what *system*, by what process, is it implemented? We can easily eliminate language. But then...how? (Let us say, to oneself?)

The end of that process might be activity, but how did the awareness arrive not only at the compelling activity, but the conscious decision to implement it? Consider that an animal can perceive sights, sounds, smells, tastes and touch. Does the animal, however, have and retain the knowledge of these perceptions to compel a reaction? That would be closer to consciousness! Unless it is instant behavioral response...reaction! Would the former require some kind of...language? Would it not require communication with oneself? Perhaps depending on the appropriateness of the response and the number of possible responses from which the animal had to choose would determine a level of consciousness...as the element of decision comes into play...and that would certainly require consciousness!

How does the knowledge of one's perceiving come about? And there is the question of memory. The retaining of all one's perceptions may constitute and contribute to the quality of one's consciousness...but in itself it is not consciousness, not awareness, only additional material and fuel for it.

At this point the question arises: if there exists no communicative facility, as, in an infant, or an animal, might it still be possible to perceive, or to perceive and be conscious of that perception? And is consciousness contingent upon an inner conception of one's perceptions with oneself? How could the outsider know?

Communication with oneself is not the only problem to be considered in pursuit of our initial question. Another entails *memory* and communication in time and space.

In a way, one aspect of memory is less complex than consciousness. Yet this is only superficially, as the two are connected. Still, let us consider the wonderful accomplishments of artificial memory: the visual preservation of the light of a physical scene, through the still camera or motion picture camera, or the aural, audio preservation, or recording of sound. Olfactory memory of smell or taste has not been accomplished, or even tried because of the ease of duplication in these areas. But how are human visual and aural memories recorded...preserved...and retrieved? Understanding initial personal and conscious recording of these sensations would seem less cryptic and complex than retrieving or accessing, recognizing and appreciating the neural images and sounds...fragrances and tastes!

Again how are they connected to awareness and consciousness...and how are the stored memories and images chronologically sorted and recognized...understood?

The answers to these questions are not resolved, but the subject matter and questions raised need to be kept in mind as we postulate and hopefully speculate our initial hypothesis.

There is, understandable speculation about a hereafter. And, there IS, without question, an answer to that speculation...as there are answers, definitive answers, to all conundrums and speculations. First, however, in honing in on the answer to the hereafter speculation, two linked peripheral puzzles and troublesome mysteries need to be addressed, One is the nature, essence and character of *consciousness*; the second, even more esoteric, complex and almost inexplicably arcane, is not merely the *essence* of awareness, but the intangible *provenance* of one's consciousness...and its subsequent likelihood, inevitability...or multiple inevitabilities!

The question of consciousness as understood and explained by Indian philosophers requires an understanding that consciousness *exists* separate from the mind and body. It goes on to elucidate a consciousness which, though existing outside the body and mind, is nonetheless pervasive and illuminating - through the mind - without which it cannot be experienced, while although still retaining its unlimited character.

The problem with understanding and examining consciousness lies in itself as subject, and as examining tool. Like light it requires itself to further investigate itself. And to examine its absence, darkness, is not possible as the light decimates the darkness. Similarly, implementing consciousness to examine itself would be required. But to illuminate its vacancy only introduces itself, defeating and decimating any initial contrasting condition.

The consciousness that hopefully confirms us to ourselves and provides the awareness of our living state... might also raise the question of the miracle of our being HERE...NOW...and not in any of the other places on the planet, nor in any of the myriad years that have gone by! How is it...that it is YOU who are perceiving this consciousness...who are aware? Is this a UNIQUE identity...of ALL the times, places and identities...it is...YOU? Or - is it possible that this is not a unique time and place? Is it possible that you have ALWAYS been...and will continue to BE?

If this IS a possibility, it seems clear that past *memory* will play no part. Memories will be wiped clean together along with physical stature, intellect, height, weight, complexion, ideas, notions opinions, perhaps even form...even human form. Only *consciousness* will remain...but again, with NO memory; though it WILL remain as the SAME (though un-characteristic and un- identifiable) strange force.

This consciousness is a continuum...uninterrupted and un-destroyed as the force that it is...simply awaiting its development and enhancement by the intellect, environment, prowess and longevity of its new host. No connection is ostensible or discerned, if even realized, as it provides the awareness that serves, yet evades and eludes its host.

As far as any other options, the probability that any one of us is uniquely existent today and will not be here again, soon, is more than billions upon billions to one.

You won't remember any of it...at ALL...but, chances are...we shall meet again!

DÉJÀ VU, DÉJÀ VU

Universe! Can you imagine it? An expanse with no end? And if there were a boundary, a terminus, what would it be like? Made of what material? What would lie beyond it? Nothing, of course...because, by definition, the boundary...the end...would be the...end! But...nothing? What is "nothing?" Well, he thought, he had the answer. Finally, he had arrived at the answer.

He paused before setting his thesis down...to reflect: The Earth...some eight thousand miles in diameter; the Sun, our nearest star, some 800,000 miles across the middle. He puffed on his pipe and watched the smoke dissipate into nothing. Nothing, he thought, the Sun was nothing compared to larger, more distant stars: Betelgeuse, at least 500 light years distant, Antares, the giant, Rigel, that blue brilliance. If Rigel were any nearer than its 850 light years we would never have night! And beyond all of these behemoths, beyond the galaxies and galactic clusters were the vast dark expansive reaches of space. But, reaching... to where? Reaching to what; stretches that would require light, traveling at more than 186,000 miles per second, billions of years to traverse? A puzzling conundrum, but he knew he had the answer. Essentially, it was simple.

Two men, one standing in front of the other. The man in the rear tells the one before him to begin walking, in a straight line. "If you keep walking straight," he tells him, "contrary to logic as it may seem, you will eventually come up behind me!"

"Impossible," says the man in front. "If I never turn to double back, I can never appear behind you." Of course, the man is unaware that the Earth is a globe and, as such, the first man's statement is true. Similarly, it is with the universe. Again, the pipe. More smoke.

Einstein posited that space is curved. What did that mean? How can you "curve" space? Well, he was not speaking of a vacuum or the "space" lying before you. Einstein was speaking of the space that comprises, the space that IS, our universe. Like our Earth, once thought of as flat, space itself, that which is the expanse of our universe, is curved.

Thus, we can explain and understand the perplexing paradox as to how the universe is finite (confined and contained) and yet INfinite (boundless and unending) at the same time! Starting at any point and proceeding in a "straight" line, on a "straight," unveering trajectory, the traveler would ultimately, after billions of light years, having reached the "boundary" of the universe, arrive at his very starting point…WITHOUT HAVING PASSED THROUGH ANY DISCERNABLE TERMINUS! Space, like the Earth, is curved!

Time, also, like space, is infinite and boundless, with no beginning and no end. "ALWAYS" is the key word. Time, as well, is CURVED!

The apparent "beginning," the "Big Bang," occurred following a compression of all matter into a kind of super black hole. Having reached a limit of mass, or "massiveness," density, and unable to contain itself, the hole explodes…with such a force and speed as to occur everywhere at once, creating the universe as we know and can see it today through all of its billions of light years of space to the receding quasars at its boundaries. But ultimately, inevitably, the recession will slow and come to a halt, followed by a collapse. At that moment all the clusters, the galaxies and the stars will begin to fall in upon themselves, to once again be transformed into the immense force and density of that familiar black hole. The "hole," of all matter…ALL matter, will become the identical point, that initial singularity it was in the "beginning" of time, until it can contain itself no longer. And it shall embark upon THE beginning again. Identically… everything exactly, exact in each detail, as it was before…and before that! We shall all meet again! Every event, every thing…the same, as it was before…as it ALWAYS was!

ALWAYS has been! The smoke dissipated once more, filling the room with a sweet fragrance. He lifted his treatise which he knew contained the answer...the words he needed to prove his theory and began reading:

"Universe! Can you imagine it? An expanse with no end? And if there were a boundary, a terminus, what would it be like? Made of what material? What would lie beyond it? Nothing, of course...because, by definition, the boundary...the end...would be the...end! But...nothing? What is "nothing?" Well, he thought, he had the answer. Finally, he had arrived at the answer.

He paused before setting his thesis down...to reflect: The Earth...some eight thousand miles in diameter; the Sun, our nearest star, some 800,000 miles across the middle. He puffed on his pipe and watched the smoke dissipate into nothing. Nothing, he thought, the Sun was nothing compared to larger, more distant stars: Betelgeuse, at least 500 light years distant, Antares, the giant, Rigel, that blue brilliance. If Rigel were any nearer than its 850 light years we would never have night! And beyond all of these behemoths, beyond the galaxies and galactic clusters were the vast dark expansive reaches of space. But, reaching... to where? Reaching to what; stretches that would require light, traveling at more than 186,000 miles per second, billions of years to traverse? A puzzling conundrum, but he knew he had the answer. Essentially, it was simple....

DREAMS

CORDOVAN

In the dream it was always the same. One pair of those deep, dark, maroon cordovan shoes, in the back of the closet. He dusts the pair and goes back to bed. Sometimes he dresses and goes out. And in his waking closet, in the back, one pair of dusted cordovans. All too often he was moved to wonder if this was not part of his dream.

The dream had become more lucid and in time he actually decided to buy an additional pair of these shoes for his closet merely to serve as markers to distinguish between this odd dream and his reality. So he invested in yet another pair of the cordovans, a little lighter in color, but essentially the same. He placed them next to the older pair in the closet. He had dinner that night and slept. There was no dream.

The next morning he rose and before anything else went to his closet. There was only one pair of cordovans. The new pair was gone. He removed some of his strewn boxes, magazine stacks and sundries, pushed back hangers of lengthy garments in case of his having misplaced the shoes, but there was no sign of them.

That night the dream came again. The closet...and the additional pair of cordovans.

He awoke in a sweat and went to his closet. One pair.

That morning he dressed and went to the shoe store. The clerk who had sold him was not in, but he was assured no cordovan shoes had been purchased for sometime. At his insistence the cashier looked through several receipts on a spike, but found no evidence of any such sale.

He could have bought another pair of the shoes right then and there but he was somehow terrified that they too would inexplicably vanish so he simply thanked the clerk and went home. It was following dinner that he went to his closet and discovered the shoes, neatly aligned, where he had placed them the day before, next to one another.

He wondered if it all was a dream, after all, and if so, what the dream would disclose that night as the two attendants in the cordovan shoes, one a lighter color than the other gently lowered him onto electro-shock table. He took hold of an old rag and prepared to dust the cordovans.

REUNION

It was in the year 2006 that the New York Friars club celebrated its 100th birthday. As part of the celebration the Friars, always coming up with innovative ideas to delight and amuse their membership, decided upon a "time capsule" that would contain and store away bits of memorabilia, tokens, mementos and trivia to re-convey, bring back and otherwise resurrect the last hundred years for the denizens of 2106.

The club had just recently opened an earlier "capsule" optimistically buried one hundred years prior on the occasion of the club's founding. The time-capsule contained snippets and small items linked to the likes of Robert Ripley (Believe it or Not), George M. Cohan, Jack Johnson, young Ty Cobb, Teddy Roosevelt, Mark Twain, and other luminaries. It contained clippings from local newspapers like The World, The Telegram, The Sun, The Herald, The Journal and The Tribune. The papers headlined major events such as the Spanish American War and the San Francisco earthquake as well as players and scenes that had long since faded from history's stage.

Now, as a portion of the more contemporary and "popular" 21st century record, and part of the "amusement" of project "time-capsule," each Friar was offered a page in the new container. It was an opportunity to provide our progeny and future Friars with his, or her, own conclusive version of…the way it was. Friar Gregory Alexson was one such Friar.

Alexson had just written a book entitled Nosebleeds From Washington Heights, a collection of twenty short tales about the people, places and events that comprised life and time in that small enclave in upper Manhattan in the 1940s and '50s.

Alexson thought highly of his little book, a candid and uncontrived compendium, replete with minutiae and details long since forgotten by all but a few of his contemporaries, most of whom were either dead or already showing signs of encroaching dementia, remembering precious few details of any people, places or events that occurred more than fifty-five years ago.

On his one page supplied by the innovators of the capsule destined for the time-trip into the year 2106 Alexson wrote: "My name is Gregory Alexson. Some one hundred years ago I wrote a book entitled Nosebleeds From Washington Heights in which I described events which took place in the Heights some one hundred fifty years ago…from when you are reading this. With due diligence, you might still find a copy of this tome in the Friars' archives. Should you be so fortunate, let us meet on these pages and I will be pleased to conduct you on my tour. Let us get to know one another. I look forward to it. Until then, I remain, Gregory Alexson.

* * *

And "remain" he might have, although that broaches on speculation. Michael Swift, a gentleman whose residence was not far from where the Friar's Club of New York still made its Monasterial base of operations had long wondered about the place, and although he was not a performer, had promised himself that one day he would make membership inquiries.

Swift was not by nature a joiner or one who sought the companionship of others (strangers or friends) but on lonesome, often vacuous weekend afternoons, when he had occasion to casually pass the Friars' establishment, often the lure of the place, its Gothic entryway and façade, beckoned to him.

These enticements were for the most part subtle and subliminal and passed unnoticed (offset perhaps by the prospects of initiation fees, dues, intricate requirements and perhaps even rejection) but often even the most daunting dissuaders are inexplicably overcome and it was on a gray Sunday evening that Michael did not pass the Monastery by, but on whimsical impulse pulled at the heavy oak door to his left and entered the Friars' premises.

Now, the Friars Club of New York, although one of the more colorful and prestigious of the many clubs and fraternal organizations that abounded in the city (The Williams Club, The Wings Club, The Players and the National Arts Club, to name a few) was much more amenable to the visitor or passer-by than say the University Club, still, in this year 2106, a block or so away on 54th Street and Fifth Avenue. For reasons known best to that organization's membership, the curious are kept well away, and turned away, and short of being escorted by a member, a non-member has no way of so much as entering the hallowed halls of that place. It is a cold and unfriendly place, almost hostile, and certainly pales, as does its membership, before the warmth, color and hospitality of the Friars Club.

When Swift navigated the few steps leading to yet another heavy door he paused before a large painting on the left wall of the entryway. A small plaque on its side noted that this oddly iridescent depiction of the club had been hanging on that very spot for more than 100 years. On the right wall hung a complicated bronze tablet with names of former Abbots, Deans, and various officials who had occupied offices of the club throughout the years.

He glanced at it, then went through the next portal leading to the reception area and the main floor of the club. The wind from the outside rushed into the club's entryway behind him as the door slowly snuffled shut.

Against the side wall on the left, a few paces beyond the drinking bar (whose name he would later learn had undergone several changes over the years) was a long glass case. Swift paused before the case and peered down into it, his gaze settling onto an array of curious looking items, most of which appeared to be documents.

"Can I be of assistance," said the neatly clad gentleman whom Swift had noticed earlier in the hallway?

"These looked interesting," said Michael. "I was considering membership in the club and passing by today I thought I would stop in."

The gentleman chose one of Michael's threads and picked up on it.

"All of what is in the case has been taken recently from our time-capsule. We just set up this display a few days ago…so your visit is timely!"

Michael pointed to one of the prominent newspaper's front pages. The date showed 2006.

"One hundred years old?"

"Exactly," said the Friar. "Some things haven't changed much... but many things have."

"How about membership requirements? Still possible?" Michael chuckled. "Affordable?"

The man "saw" his chuckle and raised him another. "We're reasonable…assuming you meet the other requirements. But they are not especially stringent or restrictive. Come up to the office and I'll get you a packet of forms." The man extended his hand. "I'm Edwin Cory."

They rode up to the fifth floor in a tiny, antiquated, elevator and then took a flight of back stairs leading to a suite of offices. Cory ducked into a cubicle and, reaching into a drawer, retrieved an envelope evidently filled with a packet of membership forms.

"You'll enjoy the club," he said, handing Michael the package, "Everyone does. When you fill out the paperwork just leave it at the front desk. I'll get it!" Michael noticed Cory's name was already printed on the envelope.

"Incidentally," Michael said, as he was about to go, "will these…ah…time-capsule pieces be out for awhile…and available to look at?" He felt drawn to the case and its contents.

"Absolutely," said Cory assuring, "everything is open to the membership specifically. And you should find a complete list of the capsule's contents in your envelope."

Swift almost expected to hear: "Have a nice day." But instead Cory said: "We hope to hear from you." Michael could hardly wait to get home.

* * *

When Michael got home he purposely avoided his electronic mailbox. It had become a scourge over the years. The days of one or two happy pieces of mail, actually co-respondence (slipped beneath the door) were long gone. The "mail" now arrived in bundles, and if you dared stay away, out of touch, as it were, with "society," you were inundated with canvas and burlap sacks awaiting your return; not just brown paper packages wrapped up with string. Ostensibly, a citizen was on a…tether; a fewer than ten day tether.

Furthermore, the daily onslaught each day, incredibly, contained assessments, advisories, premiums, warnings, notices, caveats, bills, admonitions, increases, cancellations, complications, changes, offers, advertisements, taxes, petitions, promotions, expirations, forms and statements. It was a disaster and joyless onus of depression and chagrin; a daily onslaught which brought one to despondency and near desperation. So he thought it best on this day to ignore what lay in wait for him in the mail room and proceed to the opening of a more pleasant and promising package upstairs.

He slipped inside his tiny apartment, put up a pot of real tea and opened the Friars envelope.

Michael Swift's kitchen window looked out and down 18 floors onto a shadowy city, but still was high enough to allow sunlight and fresh air into his modest apartment. The kitchen itself was no more than an island at the end of a large living room and did not foster any feelings of confinement. Behind it was his solitary bedroom, a cluster of closets, a small hallway and bathing facilities.

He carefully opened Cory's envelope, perused a brochure of photographs showing each of the Friars Club rooms, and felt an urgency to fill out the forms before him, even prior to considering costs. His strange compulsion comprised such positive and unyielding euphoria to be irresistible.

The next day Michael left his application at the club's front desk and was about to leave when Cory appeared and asked if Michael had a chance to go over any of the time capsule papers. He had not, but seemed so regretful Cory offered to seat him in a corner of the recently renamed entry floor bar to examine some of the documents over a drink on the house. The prospect was too inviting to refuse.

Seated comfortably against the club's southern wall on a window seat, Michael began to read the top page of his 100-year-old sheaf. Curiously, the submissions were common and conventional, what one might expect: names, aphorisms, dates, platitudes and regards. Many of the occupations and identities meant nothing to Michael. It was only when he came upon Gregory Alexson's page that he felt the tug of intrigue. He squared up the remaining stack, rubber banded the bundle and read through his page again, and again!

There was something that drew him about what Alexson was saying and Michael felt compelled to seek out the "Nosebleeds" book. He did not feel that the material would in any way be disappointing, nor would his excursion be a trip taken in vain. In fact, he thought, the journey would provide an excellent and perhaps rich initiation of his own creation into the Friars Club.

***

Michael was soon initiated into the Friars, and locating a copy of "Nosebleeds" proved not difficult at all. All the documents and sources alluded to in the time capsule were considerately placed on hand and readily accessible to members. Very few Friars, however, actually seemed to avail themselves of the material. It was unknown to most members, that officers of the club in 2006, showing great foresight and enthusiasm, had sealed all related source documents in a separate time container to be opened and made available to the membership in 2106 subsequent to the opening of the time capsule. A fresh, new looking copy of "Nosebleeds" was on file in the club's administration office.

Michael zealously pored over the book in the club's reading room and got a reasonably clear idea of what Alexson was trying to convey. The prose was so detailed and colorful Michael had moments where he felt he was not only journeying through the places in Washington Heights that Alexson described, but had actually been there. He had not.

It was after several days spent reading the book and carefully completing several of the short stories that Michael Swift had a series of dreams.

On more than one occasion he dreamed he had been invited to a Friars Club function. Entrance to the club was for him an infrequently used side door, which led down a long flight of brightly lit stairs. At the bottom of the flight, a door on his right opened to an immense banquet hall with hundreds of people milling around buffet and banquet tables. The room was decorated and painted in reds and oranges. The overall feeling and mood of the dream was a pleasant one, warm, expectant.

This dream was often coupled with two or three others, which, for some vague reason Michael began to feel had an arcane connection to the stories he was reading in the Alexson book.

One of the stories he read was told from a 14-year-old's point of view. In the story a friend's older sibling weaved tales of fantasy which, in the boys' hours of need, served to comfort them, gave them courage and, reinforced the image of the hero for both the youngsters and the teller of the tales.

It was soon after reading this particular story that Swift had what he began to feel were the first of a series of dreams specifically related to Alexson's book.

In his initial night's excursion Michael is in a place identified, in the dream, as "his old neighborhood." He is tossing a small football with an older man, about 40. The man is heavyset, dressed nicely in a brown leisure suit, and although he seems like a father figure, is only, a neighbor from the opposite side of the street. The ball is tossed back and forth, Michael does not want to miss catching it, and somehow he does not miss it. The man then throws a very hard and straight pass as Michael thinks he must not fumble this pass at all costs and indeed, although the football rams itself into his chest, he does not. But then, attempting to return the ball, it shoots off to another player in the street. Michael apologizes, explaining that he had thought the missile was a much larger, regulation size football.

It was, however, only after two other dreams, these apparently related to a story called The Park, (about the author's mother and the guilt he felt over a lost scarf that Michael began to recognize a connection between the dreams and the stories.

In the first of these two journeys, Michael's mother and her son are strolling on a boardwalk, to the left of which is a large department store, a combination of Macy's and F.W. Woolworth. The pair walks into the place and examines the wares only to discover that some fifteen paces or so into the store there are no lights and the aisles are dark. A clerk assures them, however, it is "alright" and one would still be allowed to shop even though it is dark inside. Michael tells his mother she may go ahead, he will wait and meet her outside. She begins to examine items on counters nearby as he loiters within watching as his mother fails to venture into the dark part of the store. He does not go outside.

It was not, however, until Michael had his second dream that he saw a distinct link to this story. At the printed tale's end, there was a photo of Michael's mother and the author as a child. The photo was taken on a street before what appeared to be a bus stop. It seemed very familiar to Swift, but he could not place it and for all he knew that specific site might no longer even exist.

This second of these two dreams seemed to Michael strongly to deal with this particular location. He is waiting for a bus somewhere in the 150s block of Washington Heights on the way downtown. It is very cold and getting late. Above Michael is an arch. Behind him is a wall. It is apparent that the place is a transfer point for the bus that will bring him home. The blowing wind is chilly. The bus is late in coming. The waiting station is white with heavy shadows.

When he awoke from this dream, he had more than the often strange and eidetic impression that accompanies a lucid dream. Michael felt that without a doubt he HAD been to this odd and shadowy place and WAS, in fact, the little boy in the photograph! It shook him and filled him with no little compulsion to find the location.

For the first time in his life he ventured to Washington Heights but could not find anyplace remotely resembling the area in the photo, nor, on reading the story several times over, could he garner a clue as to the whereabouts of the arch and the wall. Yet the sense that it did exist disturbed him beyond just the story and the photograph. He resonated with more than obsession. The perception of the place haunted him.

The Friars club itself began to take on for him a very special and ethereal aspect. Swift was seen in the place almost daily, tucked away in one of the club's reading areas poring over "Nosebleeds," his notes, maps of the Heights and Alexson's hundred-year-old time capsule page. He also thought casually many times where the staircase and banquet room of his Friars Club dream might have been. He never located it until one afternoon, after having the dream once more. He had been unable to discover the source of the dream because images in dreams are often inverted, not only in space but in time, size, color and direction. The staircase Michael had so often envisioned in his sleep was on a different side of the club, originating at a different place than he might have expected, leading to a different area, going off in a different direction and carried with it an altogether different mood than the one he'd experienced in his dream. Yet it was the same staircase. He was certain of it.

It was during a chance conversation with one of the club's older members that Michael learned the staircase indeed had once led to a banquet room many years ago, and only recently took on its new function and configuration. Things at the Friars Club, he was told, were always changing.

Michael became obsessed with why Alexson had written this deeply personal and loving manuscript. Why would he care if anyone should read it in 100 years? And why should any reader have more than a passing interest in it. Although the stories were replete with thematic and moral material, much of what they described, the specific details, the keys, certainly the players were no longer extant. But why did he feel differently? Why did he sense a distinct connection to the material? Why did he feel involved in this manuscript, in these stories? The answer was: if he were writing for himself! Some years earlier Michael had given up writing a novel, justifying his abandonment with the excuse that chances of agents or publishers even looking at his manuscript with an eye toward publication were more than slim. In fact, he quipped wryly, his chances were better not even entering his book in the market arena. A close friend had once told him he seemed to be missing the point. The "point" being, in the words of his friend: "You write for yourself."

That night Michael had two connecting dreams: In the first, he is in a giant cube…a matrix of open rail-less stairwells and pathways within which he is able to climb, jump and wend his way across and down. He progresses on the downward trek, relatively unimpeded except for time and effort. Then, in a small, seemingly crammed, labyrinthine neighborhood keeping with the aspect of cubes and angles, laden with twists and maze-like paths, he is to meet with his father. The meeting is to take place somewhere in the maze, but Michael feels he may have gone too far. He asks directions and is pointed back in the direction from which he came. Michael realizes he must double back and go far out of his way to arrive at the meeting place with his father. A long, giant flight of stairs presents itself but he avoids this and finds his father at the appointed place. The two of them look through store windows in the street. The stores boast appealing tarts and rare items, but Michael and his father are in an unexplained hurry. They pass a newsstand in crossing to the other side of town. Michael looks longingly at the items on the newsstand but buys nothing. His father seems not to be annoyed at him for being detained.

In the second dream Michael is seated on a stone/marble bench opposite three other people. This seems to have followed some kind of sea "accident." The floor of what presents itself to be an island after the group's being adrift and lost is made of some kind of ceramic tile. Michael announces that while the others remain seated he will scout out the surroundings and perhaps find help. Embarking on this mission he sees as far as he can that the place is perfectly flat, the ground is of marble and ceramic tile, populated by hundreds of people clothed in togas and similar Roman garb. There are NO buildings or shops, but as he walks among the pedestrians he has a contented, elated feeling and is eager to mix among these people and meet them. Although nothing other than the wandering people is in evidence, Michael suspects there IS something to be found and satisfying connections to be made. Soon he seems to lose interest in his companions but does not feel as if they will be forsaken and eventually will reunite. He is not compelled to return to the bench and instead experiences great joy and well being. There are no threats, loneliness nor fears. And although no one speaks to him, the people seem friendly and smile. There is no end to the immaculately clean, white, plaza. To the horizon, the uniform and ubiquitous ceramic and marble tile is visible. He speculates that this is not unlike being on a grid but he is unaware that this is actually the case.

The Bronx no longer existed when Michael went seeking Gun Hill Road, nor did any of the other locales cited in "Nosebleeds:" Narrowsburg, Union City, Pennsylvania Station or Highbridge. Yet

Michael knew he had been there and was beginning to become convinced he had lived through the stories carried on the words describing and chronicling these places. And then after his final rereading of the Nosebleeds tales he had a night filled with yet another pair of vivid dreams.

Actually, the dreams came on two successive nights. And although the subject matter seemed to be separate, each of the dreams were connected to its counterpart and appeared as one. On Wednesday Michael dreamed he was on a bus with a friend. They get off on the outskirts of what appeared to be a forsaken or abandoned town. The friend goes on ahead while Michael lags behind, indicating that he will catch up and join his friend in the morning. He walks the town alone all night and into the early morning hours, along dusty roads. He learns the name of the place is Springton and finds it is very much like an old camp. A few stands surround the center of the town, with some merchants selling merchandise, but most are asleep standing or leaning on their wooden booths. Others, mostly men, sleep on the ground in sleeping bags or blankets. Michael wonders how he will ever find his friend and thinks how stupid and thoughtless his earlier idea was. As he walks he calls out his friend's name in panic and there, on the rim of a little hill he sees him, just having awakened from whatever berth *he* had found overnight. The reunion is comforting, reassuring and a confirmation of the security he had originally felt when starting out alone on his initial walk.

Suddenly the scene dissolves and morphs into a hotel room. Michael and his friend go "downstairs" and appear in a large showroom with many maze-like cubicles. In each are counters and shelves displaying products. Michael stops at one selling only red products. They are labeled "Old Spice." He tries a sample but it does not smell like Old Spice, and the label is missing two of the letters. Still, although it says: "Original" it does not smell like the original. Outside this showroom it is somehow understood Michael and his friend could avail themselves of anything they wish, but they take nothing. The sky is extremely blue and the architecture is modern, interesting, pleasant and different. Again, it is stark white stucco. There are only very short and narrow walls and many arches. Everything is open and connects. Many people mill around and Michael asks where this is but no one seems to know. He stops children and asks "what city are we in?" But they do not know. Through one arch he can see a girl demonstrating a product. The girl looks familiar. Michael senses that she is part of the "administration." She behaves as if she knows him and they chat amicably. Conspiratorially he asks her where he is. She produces a paper and pen, chides him not to tell anyone, and writes down a strange name. She says it is somewhere east of the Bahamas.

It was on Thursday that his final night voyage came. He dreamed of a "camp" as word is announced that "camp" is over. A fellow camper passes on the way out of a waiting room area and asks Michael to join him. He is indifferent, robust and apparently in good health. Michael refuses and the man appears displeased but continues on his way. When Michael leaves the area on his own he finds himself in a hallway of his old public school. A few women are convening and he fears they might prevent him from using the exclusive front door exit. The women are pleasant and do not interfere with this. Once outside Michael turns to the east and laments that it is only across the street that there is a bus route, although he is consoled that there are many people waiting on a line for the bus. It is then that he realizes indeed his next appointment lies not on the eastside, but on the Westside, only farther downtown, and he can take the bus. Michael is delighted at this epiphany and heads toward the queue of people. He does not mind the long line and anticipates sitting comfortably on this downtown bus even though it does not have far to go.

Seated on the bus Michael Swift finds himself trying to puzzle out the meaning of his dream when he realizes the "camp" was part of "college."

He is then transformed into a clown and skates to a window in the bus as his attention is focused on a Pixie in a garden. "Listen to the Pixie," he implores himself. "The Pixie will make a revelation and will clarify everything." Michael waits for the truism. And the Pixie, from its perch in a tree, says: "The passage of time, that's all we can do." The passage of time…is all we can do!"

That was on Friday morning. Friday there was no sign of Michael Swift at the Friars Club, no record of his membership application, no indication of him at all. The book *Nosebleeds from Washington Heights* was back on the administration office shelf with several other papers. All documents from the time capsule were in the display case. Edwin Cory denied ever hearing of Michael Swift. In fact, the question never came up!

DIMENSIONS

SHADE

Sometime ago there was a wonderful place just south of Bleecker Street on Sixth Avenue in New York's Greenwich Village called Welcome to New York. It was wonderful because it housed thousands of old photographs, maps, pieces of memorabilia and assorted tidbits having to do with a New York City long gone. You could spend an entire afternoon rummaging through the many shelves and bins in this emporium until your feet ached and you needed to visit a restroom. But the very dust in the place was wonderful.

I don't think I'd ever emerged from a visit to this dark little shop without bags of things, envelopes of photographs, books, postcards and odd maps of people, places and institutions that no longer existed. I had always overspent, far beyond what I had intended, often pointlessly, and my fingers were filthy as a result of handling the hundred plus year old merchandise. The treasures to be discovered, uncovered, buried, in this shop's cabinets and on her tables were endless and unknown until excavated.

It was a joy to get home with these parcels and to unload the lot, the likes of which, despite the ripe age of any item, probably had not been seen by too many people aside from a few inveterate collectors of New Yorkiana! There were rare post cards, photos, cartoons and linens, of Coney Island and her Steeplechase, Eight by Tens of the 1939 World's Fair, the last good time before WWII, glossies of the crowds at Yankee Stadium in its heyday, as well as original shots of bygone city eateries, hotels, buildings and streets; all from a forgotten era. Much of the material spoke of products vanished, as well as the advertisements boasting of those miracle items no longer extant. And, of course, there were the trinkets; buttons, badges, pins and assorted souvenirs. And on a rare day you found something even rarer, more arcane, more of an esoteric surprise than you anticipated. This was one such day.

Aside from subway maps and booklets showing stops where today's trains, busses and trolleys no longer stopped, and charts of a city quite evolved with designations that were now not only no longer used, but considered quite inappropriate (such as "asylums") there were those rare shots of New York's infamous and dark Third Avenue Elevated line; rare because it was too physically dim to photograph easily, but also spiritually dark with few surroundings other than taverns, pawn shops and shadows. This cheerless configuration was taken down in the 1960's with very little remaining to remind the tourist or native of that chilly gloom. And there were also photos of the city's other, earlier, elevated, now decimated, structures on sixth, ninth and second avenues.

Throughout the historical hovel there were bits of the past...pictures of crowds of only men...and only men wearing hats; gentlemen nicely dressed in shirts and ties, ladies in finery, dresses and heels, stereographic photos where images of the city would leap out at the viewer through its housing stereopticon into all three dimensions, and a fantastic set of photographs revealing either new and crisply detailed likenesses of original advertisements painted on buildings or the faded remains of those depictions. (Often these remnants were so faint that discerning the original ad was nearly impossible, but trying, or seeking a photo of the fresh original, made for an interesting pastime.) There before you on some obscure street where a building had recently been torn down, adjacent to it, stood revealed, on a five story wall, the flecks of what once was...a bright, garish message...today, quite indiscernible. But, there on one of Welcome to New York's dusty bins, was a clear, sharp, 8x10 glossy of the original advertisement: "Dutch Boy...Lead Based Paint," "Broadway Central Hotel," "Mail Pouch Tobacco" or "Hotel San Rafael." There were the billboards surrounding the neatly clad crowd of all men, (hats, white shirts, ties and vests) circling Yankee

Stadium: "Drink Canada Dry" "Vat 69" "Call For Phillip Morris" "Brushless Burma Shave" and "Calvert Whiskey."

And when you looked at the glossies of the frolicking boys and girls at the 1939 World's Fair, you had to wonder how many of these boys were destined to disappear into the future darkness of WWII never to return.

It was on one such excursion to Welcome to New York that I came upon two spectacularly sharp and detailed daguerreotypes. The pictures were taken from one of the towers of the Metropolitan Life building in downtown Manhattan. They were of nothing in particular but I fell in love with their age and clarity. They cried out for closer scrutiny and examination. I thought perhaps I could find the buildings which preceded my current lodgings and perhaps, with sufficient magnification, some of those original building sign paintings. The two photographs were outrageously expensive but I had to have them.

Because of the great height from which they were taken and the incredible clarity defining the detail and overwhelming density of the city the images somehow seemed worth their price, and, part of that worth was also because of the challenge I felt accompanied each; the wealth of available information in each exposure.

It was on the following morning I examined each piece carefully with a powerful loupe. The detail was extraordinary and I thought I was able, after some time, to locate the exact avenue and cross street of where I now had my residence. In its place, though not nearly as tall, was large tenement, some of whose side windows faced the camera's lens. I carefully studied the view from what seemed to be the perspective of the window I thought might eventually have been mine until I was convinced that was more than a possibility! And it was after more than two hours I thought I discerned what appeared to be a shadow through the open window. I got a stronger loupe and pored over the photograph until my eye began to smart. The quality of the photograph was so perfect and its grain so fine the sharpness of the image persisted through my staring and separation or distortion of the pixels hardly occurred. Again, the shape and image of what gave the appearance of a shadow presented its distinct outline. It could have been a person looking directly at the camera lens.

Throughout the afternoon and evening I studied my photo, consulting additional maps and charts of the city that year. I cross referenced with other pictures to triangulate and home in on the street. Although none of the photographs were as sharp and distinctly detailed as my daguerreotype the area seemed the same but I had no similar view of that window. It was on the next morning something strange occurred.

I took the loupe and the image, which I now protected with a piece of clear, thin, Lucite and tabs for gripping the corners and, setting the magnifier comfortably in front of my eye I found myself to be taking an inordinate bit of time to locate my window. After a few minutes of repetitious and frustrating circling about the photograph I removed the loupe and repositioned it. It was then I noticed the most shocking and disturbing image I could scarcely believe. I can only surmise, to this day that it has always been so, and that somehow I must initially have missed it. But behind what I had taken to be my window, someone had drawn a shade. No number of re-examinations of the photo has since afforded me the original image which I thought I had seen in that particular area.

It was not until agonizing and obsessing over this inexplicable development I thought to consult my old friend, the proprietor of the shop, Welcome to New York. I had hoped that, in his knowledge and familiarity with his stock, he would surely recall and be able to confirm if, in fact, what I was seeing had always existed. Perhaps it was through some optical mishap or mis-focusing I had simply overlooked the shade…or taken it for something else…or, through some aberration, something had gone awry with whatever elements made up this strange photo. Or, perhaps, he would indicate that was *not* the case. But the idea of bringing this enigma to my friend comforted me and assuaged my anxieties... somewhat.

So it was that the very next morning, I wrapped the image carefully in several layers of protective paper and backed it with cardboard and placed the entire business in an envelope.

I took the "D" train to Waverly Place and proceeded to Bleecker at Sixth Avenue. When I crossed over to where Welcome to New York had always made its home I noticed the banner which had always flown, flapping over the shop was gone. The place was closed. It was no longer. A shade was drawn over the window and the door.

That welcome oasis was never to open again. The little shop itself was now a relic of yesterday whose old and cool waters of the past would never again refresh the harried traveler through today. Now, little draws me down to that peculiar area of New York City, and I remain at home, only occasionally taking out the old sharp and clear daguerreotype to examine it one final time. But I do spend many hours peering out of my window over the city, watching. And there are days when I would swear; on the far horizon, I see a glimmer of light; A flicker in the distance. It is then that I simply draw the shade.

QUADRHOM

He was, for as long as he could recall, fascinated by distances and shapes. Dimensions. Most of what he read never failed to cite Edwin Abbott's Flatland...(somewhat more than a one dimensional tale). But rarely had cosmologists, mathematicians, physicists and quantum theorists managed to go beyond, at least *get* beyond, the three spatial and the one time extension of...our existential frame. There was one noteworthy day, however: A few miles east, several north, 18 floors up, at quarter past two in the afternoon.

Yes there was Abbot, Greene, and Kaku, all trying to convey the unimaginable, analogously; trying to draw parables, but necessarily using lines, forms and objects from our own experience. When the analogy was completed, however, the metaphor laid out was, of course, comprised of lines, planes and cubes which, in *time* as well, was... only the familiar 4D construct.

What the theorists and writers suggested was, at best, a depiction of how additional dimensions might simply be hidden from our perceptions; as they took pride in expressing: "folded in upon themselves." What gave credibility to these positions was the mathematics which not only seemed to substantiate the extra dimensions, but which actually led to them and required them.

For example: one might envision a high, suspended, wire, aloft some distance away. The distant image of the wire would appear to a grounded observer to represent only the single dimension of length. A line. Upon closer examination however, let us say, atop this wire, as revealed to a tiny creature crawling across, or even through it, the dimensions of width and thickness would be apparent. The theorists opined that even smaller creatures would experience more than the width and depth <u>not earlier apparent</u> to the distant observer but, if tiny enough, the microscopic observer might even come upon the several extra dimensions extant deep in the strange recesses of our space (perhaps even deep in the recesses of time as well).

Go figure that one. What seems always overlooked is that all these observations would still be made from… here…in 4D, within, and from, our space and time… unless we were utilizing yet another dimension of which, of course, we were so far unaware.

Going through some put-together and take-apart puzzles he had collected over the years Greer came upon a unit in a clear container he had forgotten all about. It was sealed. A gift he had never opened…or one he had impulsively purchased and tucked away. The figure was comprised of four wooden pieces, each of which had six adjoining edges, while the entire unit had six inner faces, twelve outer sides, thirty six edges and twelve inner magnets which held the form together. It was called Quad Rhom.

Dodecahedron? Icosahedron? No, the icosahedron would have to have twenty triangular faces. The dodecahedron would have the twelve plane faces…but each face of this unit was a diamond, not a pentagram. And the midpoint, at the joining of each tri-diamond section, was what might have been the corner of a cube glanced at from an angle facing the cube's edge, not its side.

The base corners of each *apparent* cube were what joined to the other units with each of the removable sections abutting the other two, connecting all six outer sides. (Only three sides of any *apparent* cube could be viewed at any time.) The rest of the cube, the other three faces, receded to become one with the non-existent façade of its adjacent neighbors, or as they might be more correctly called, components of a rhombi dodecahedron!

There are, strangely, in our universe, so far as we know, only five Platonic Solids. Dimensions and Platonic Solids, thought Greer, would seem to be related. And it occurred to him that six or more Platonic

Solids would simply require an extra dimension. But, he thought, if one more dimension could allow another polyhedron, perhaps stumbling upon or creating even the design or configuration of a sixth polyhedron might at least reveal the way to a fourth spatial dimension.

The makers of this novelty advised that the Quad Rhom would lead the way to discovering a spatial fourth dimension, ensconced in nature's geometry.... Could it be the tiny, spatially ensconced Calabi Yau...the speculated one of ten tiny configurations noted in string theory?

In a small pamphlet included with the Quad Rhom it is noted that a line ninety degrees from length measures width; an extension ninety degrees from that brings us to height or depth. But the rhombi dodecahedron, according to the pamphlet's authors, can be extended into four directions or dimensions!

The writers instructed Quad Rhom owners to open the unit and count the number of edges that meet at the center. These four lines, they further explained, lay an equal distance from one another and represent THE four directions of the 4D system!

Well, thought Greer, we had a definition. A path, perhaps, but nothing uniquely observable. Then, the instructions went on, however, to say: "Turn your Quad Rhom *inside out* and hold it together so all the magnets face out. You will see that three new blocks could be added to each block...to make four new Quad Rhoms nested together." Finally the writers explained how this could continue forever and form the matrix of a spatial 4D system.

Greer opened his unit as described and lay its sections equally distant and apart from one another but found he was unable to "turn" the Quad "inside out," as the magnets in the instructed position seemed to repel each other. Nor could they remain arranged in any symmetrical formation. He placed them as best he could at last, with only one of the Quad's sections just slightly askance from its neighbors.

Scrutinizing the strange formation and imagining the extended design as the promised venue to a "4D System" Greer recalled a childhood love affair that he enjoyed with a crystal bauble his seamstress grandmother had given him as a child. It was bluish and tear-dropped shaped, through which, staring at a good light source, young Greer was able to distinguish what he clearly made to be a desert landscape. As his one eye peered at the light source through the bauble he could clearly discern several footprints in the sparking sand. They were so bright and clear as to leave a breathless Greer scouring the bluish landscape for minutes on end, awaiting a life form to appear. None ever did but each time he gazed through the bauble, the landscape and its strange footprints never failed, not merely to fascinate, but also to have changed somewhat. The changes left him so indelibly curious he carried his bauble as a charm for years.

Now, inexplicitly he retrieved it and, once again, gazed through it. The light was less than the best, when he had rested on his bed staring through the bauble at the overhear light. So he pointed it about, at the Quad Rhom on the floor, when it slipped from his fingers to hit one of the jutting wooden segments. The outward facing pieces moved slightly to straighten themselves and their adjacent neighbors when all four sections snapped together to form a perfect design resembling one face of a 4D tesseract...but as if only a part of it could be discerned...on an angle.

The blue crystal bauble came to rest exactly in the center of the arrangement and the four wooden pieces of the Quad Rhom seemed to take on a new shape...a new identity. And it was only with great difficulty one could imagine these pieces as segments of the Quad Rhom, as they now embodied the shape and design of something different and compellingly unique.

And, oddly, if one looked carefully at the new arrangement formed by the two oak and two walnut pieces, one would certainly be aware of several unmistakable shadows appearing and criss- crossing the construct every few moments. Had Greer seen this he would have been gratified and impressed. But he was nowhere to be seen. He was... gone.

MIRROR, MIRROR

In a small dank basement room beneath all the ruckus of the New York Institute of Technology the two men huddled, one with his hands covering and rubbing his face. Hair mussed. The other staring at him, pointing to a diagram he was holding.

"I tell you it makes sense," he said. "It's got to work, because the numbers work. Why can't we give it a try? What's to lose?"

The man who had been rubbing his face ran his fingers through his mousy hair.

"What's to lose is time, time and face. This is silly, Harold. You've spent too much time on this already. I'm telling you, I simply can't do it. The administration won't allow it." He picked up the wax paper holding the remains of his lunch and folded it over his half eaten chicken salad sandwich, stuffing it back into the brown paper bag. "Now I've seen your idea, I've given you my opinion…"

"But you *are* the administration, Isaiah. They'll do whatever you say; whatever you recommend!" There was a moment's pause. "Just get me the equipment then," said Harold. "You won't have to take part in the experiment. All I need now is another two mirrors and the recorders. Come on, Isaiah. It won't be any trouble for you….None at all!"

"It isn't the mirrors or the electronics, Harold; it's the support, your salary, keeping you on the faculty."

"What? What do mean, Isaiah? I have tenure here. They can't let me go!"

Isaiah pulled his gleaming gold pocket watch from his vest and glowered at the time. "It's getting late," he said. "Really, Harold, we've discussed this before. I have a meeting. I have to go."

"I've given years to this university, Isaiah. It's time for them to give back. I'm not asking for much. I won't be treated like this. Please...." Harold held his hands out in entreaty.

"I'll speak to you tomorrow, Harold, tomorrow." Isaiah turned to exit the heavy door of the small basement hovel. It slammed behind him, leaving Harold to himself.

He looked into the new mirror he had purchased for his experiments. His gaunt reflection stared back. The mirror was too new. It would do for part of the project but he would eventually need something larger...older. He lifted his gaze toward the sound system's speakers; sensitive enough, but not an integral part of what he had in mind. Not yet. For now, it was the mirrors that concerned him. Harold sealed the cracks around the door and pulled the black shade over the little dusty basement window which led into nothing better lit than a subterranean closet. Then he doused the light. Blackness. Harold stood quietly for a moment, then tried to see his own hand. He could not.

They wouldn't believe him, but Harold knew that if one could achieve *total* darkness but still get the surface of a mirror to emit light,...but never mind. They wouldn't listen. No one had ever done it before. The secret lay in the use of two reflective surfaces, *exactly* positioned. They hadn't used two mirrors. It was a reverberation principle. Each of the facing mirrors would reflect the image off the other, intensifying what little light there was; magnifying it! It would be old light. Trapped light! *The key*, Harold thought to himself, was that *not all the light off old images was reflected*. Some of the image's light was seized, trapped in the mirror. The light, now, would be coming from *within* the mirror; from its depths. And there was no telling what that would reveal. *Foolish people*, thought Harold. *They don't understand. They cannot fathom the significance of my work.*

When Isaiah returned the next day there was a dank odor about the small room. And it was dark.

"Harold? Are you here, Harold?"

There was no answer.

"Harold?" cried Isaiah. "It's me. I brought you some coffee."

Isaiah detected a slight movement in the corner where light had trickled in from behind the open door. Harold bounded up, off his little stool.

"Isaiah," he said, in a chilling whisper, "you know String Theory: the tiniest particles…the building blocks of all matter…so called strings? Nothing more than vibrations? Cannot be halved? Cannot be reduced? Nonsense, Isaiah! How can they reflect light if they are smaller than light particles? They are *larger* than light particles! Photons are the building blocks! It is light itself that we are created from. *Light* is the essence of it all. The Bible, Isaiah. The Bible! Let there be Light! *This*…is our very essence!"

Isaiah removed the lids from the cardboard coffee containers and walked toward Harold. "You've been working hard, Harold. Have some of this. I can get us some lunch if you like."

"You don't understand Isaiah. All those years I spent studying holograms. The same image over and over, whole, intact, no matter how many pieces it is broken into! The answer to it all is in the light. All of it need not be reflected. Some remains caught. Trapped in the mirrors. It is our essence, the essence of all things… and I can get it out! We can *see* it. Think of it Isaiah. Light from the ages! Images that would have been forever lost captured in the glass…but now, we can extract them! The dead can be resurrected!"

Isaiah held the coffee out to Harold who did not seem to see him.

"Isaiah, take a simple hologram and break it in two…in three pieces. What do you have? Three identical, intact holograms. Break each one of *them*, what do you have? More *complete* holograms. Replication!

They cannot be divided. The light cannot be halved. A basic particle, an essential building block cannot be halved…cannot be reduced. And the particles of light that are trapped in these mirrors are whole…! Like holograms. And we shall see, we shall bring into being, the whole image!"

"Harold," said Isaiah, "take the coffee. Let me get you some lunch. You've been hard at it."

"No Isaiah. I want you to understand first. Like the sound waves and the images we send into space…they go on and on, Isaiah…for eternity! It's conservation of energy. Bits of light that never die…are never lost! They remain in the glass…forever; until I will extract them! It starts with the light already in the glass…. It is reflected into the other mirror…and picked up, intensified by the first, and on and on, until we see it for what it is. The *entire* image! I won't let them stop my work, Isaiah! I can't let them!"

"You don't have to, Harold. I'll help you. Listen to me," Isaiah took out his gold watch. The mirror caught the image. "It's getting late, let me go and get us something. I won't be a few moments."

"No, Isaiah." Harold lifted the heavy lamp by his side and struck Isaiah with its bronze base. Isaiah fell, the burning coffee airborne for an instant, then splashing down on his tweed jacket. "No Isaiah, you aren't going anywhere anymore."

Harold dragged Isaiah's limp corpse outside the basement room door that stood ajar and down to the cellar furnace. With no little difficulty he opened the furnace door and sat Isaiah on the edge. Then he pushed his body into the oven's white hot flames. With a final twist of his shoe and leg, he shoved Isaiah into the blaze and shut the small cast iron hatch to the furnace.

Back in his cellar hovel, Harold closed the door and knelt down to mop up the spilled coffee and the droplets of Isaiah's blood. It was then, from his speakers he heard a sound. The reverberation units has been set up to detect sound from the mirrors…if that were to come to pass. At first, indiscernible, the sound became clearer: "It's getting late."

Harold looked up. It was then he saw the gleam in the mirror. The speakers sounded louder still. "It's getting late!"

The gleam in the mirror was suddenly more than light…it was Isaiah's gold pocket watch! And the face behind it mouthed the words: "It's getting late!"

Harold stood. He faced the long mirror. "No, you can't," he said…"you won't stop me." He lunged at the image in the glass with the base of his lamp which was still within his reach. The mirror shattered, fragments darting and lacerating, cutting, leaving shards of glass strewn all about the dark room.

Each piece of glass bore the full image of a man holding a gold watch…until the light from the open door filtered in and vanquished it. The phrase on the speakers became an intolerable squawk as the images faded, bound for eternity…while Harold's sliced and bleeding body lay amid the shards, thinking, "it's getting late….. It's getting late."

THE FUTURE

SECURITY

Something seemed odd as Bernie made his way through the usual afternoon crush of nannies and kids, down the flagstone ramp and into his upper east side residence. It was one of the larger apartment structures in Manhattan, and as of late, home to a vast assortment of internationals but Bernie never expected anything quite like this. Two men and two women stood blocking access to the four elevators, standing perpendicular to them. Behind them a uniformed armed guard was poised before each elevator.

"Line up quietly, please," one of the women instructed, as the nannies obediently took their places on the cue. Bernie heard muttering in several foreign accents questioning what the new procedure was all about as children in carriages began to fidget; some sensing a new and uncomfortable course ahead started to cry.

"Please empty your bags here," said a stout woman behind a large table off to the left, "and the contents of your pockets in the tray you will be given." Someone from the back of the line near the lobby's entrance was making his way down the line, distributing little plastic trays. "Do not keep your keys or wallets, please. Everything goes in the tray." The children began wailing in earnest. "Your possessions will be returned as soon as they are examined. As soon as you have done this, remove your shoes. If you have any difficulty you may use the benches against the wall, but you may lose your place on line." And the woman beckoned to the first person on line to step forward. "Do you have ID, please," she said.

The woman had been watching the others and had her belongings on her tray, but seemed puzzled. "No English," she said to the matron.

"Step to the side, please. Just wait here." With a firm hand on the perplexed lady's shoulder, the security person turned to one of the men at the far elevator and called: “Steve, please deal with this.” Steve took the woman and her pocketbook to a new table just being set up in front of the far elevator and began looking through the bag’s contents. Then they both disappeared through a service entrance door and a new man appeared at the far elevator.

“Will those with proper ID and shoes off, please line up here and all others step to your right behind the arch.” As the people began arranging themselves the security woman commenced wanding the nannies and the few tenants arriving early from work or home for any variety of reasons. Bernie stepped out of line and turned to leave the building. A new, burly man was taking his place in front of the arch which had only a few moments earlier been wheeled in. “Sir...sir...where are you going, please?” said the stout woman, calling to Bernie and pointing her finger at the lobby door.

“None of your fucking business, you fat bitch,” Bernie mumbled under his breath.

“You can’t leave here, sir, once you’re in the building.”

“Go fuck yourself, lady,” said Bernie, his volume unchecked this time.

“Steve!” called the woman, once again. And Steve, magically appearing, alone now, burst into the lobby area, from the elevators taking long, determined strides.

Catching up to the departing tenant, Steve said, “Can’t leave, sir. Sorry.”

“Who says so?” said Bernie.

“TSA, sir. It’s for your own security.”

“I don’t give a shit about security. We have enough security here. I’m going up!”

Steve whipped out a small hand-held device and pressed a button. “Problem,” he said into it and two men in purple jackets appeared, taking hold of Bernie, one on each arm.

“Come with us sir.” one of the purple men intoned. And it looked as if tenant Bernie, of the 9th floor was on his way, instead, to perhaps convene with the woman who had “no English.”

The TSA woman stepped forward and addressed the growing crowd. “We want you to be safe here. We want you to enjoy a safe, uneventful, trip on each of your elevators, to each of your final destinations. We need to make sure you are who you say you are and we don’t want anyone to be transporting anything unsafe on these elevators or with the potential of causing harm on the way to your destination floor or your apartment. In the future, as of today, you will not be permitted to be carrying anything sharp or metallic on these elevators and must finish all beverages in the lobby before boarding the elevator. All children in carriages must be strapped in and all ambulatory children must wear protective helmets. Please make sure you press your correct floor and do not attempt to leave the elevator on the wrong floor. Should this occur, and for your safety and the safety of your fellow passengers and tenants you will be brought back down and you will need to go through the entire screening process all over again. Thank you for living here, and enjoy your rides. Incidentally, starting next week, these procedures will be carried out on each floor and all hallways of the building. Again, this is for your own protection. Have a nice day.”

Those few on the line who knew him began chanting: “Bernie, Bernie, Bernie, Bernie,” but Steve began taking what seemed to be purposeful strides toward the crowd and the lobby grew quiet once more.

PASSWORD

Lawrence rode the elevator in his building down to the lobby where he traversed the grand hall to grasp the brass handle on the door to the outside. It was locked. As he jiggled the latch, and push-pulled, the uniformed doorman appeared. “Password, Mr. Chumly,” he said.

“Oh,” said Lawrence. Sorry, I forgot,” and he whispered the word.

“Thank you,” said the doorman, and he held the door open for Lawrence.

The traffic came to a stop when the light changed and Lawrence hurried across the street and down the few steps into the neighborhood grocer.

“Hi, Harry,” he said. “Just a bread and a small milk.” Harry leaned in.

“Password,” he said.

“All I need is a bread and milk,” said Lawrence.

“Sorry,” said Harry. “You know how it is. I’ve got to have the word.”

“This is ridiculous, Harry. But ok.” Larry whispered the word.

“Sorry, Mr. C. Wrong word.”

“What?” exclaimed Larry.

“The password is incorrect,” said Harry.

“Come on, Harry, I just changed it last week.”

It’s the wrong password, Mr. C.” said Harry. “I can’t give you the milk and bread!”

Lawrence rushed out of the little store and jogged up to the corner. A bus was just pulling into the stop. Larry hopped aboard and dipped his card in the box. Red letters lit the readout: "PASSWORD," they said. The driver leaned in. Larry muttered something.

"Sorry, sir," said the driver."Incorrect password."

"Oh, come on," said Lawrence. "This is getting silly. Anyway, I just paid."

"Doesn't matter, sir, I need to hear the password."

"Hey," said Larry, "screw you." And he jumped off the bus.

"Visit us online, at Bus.com," said the bus driver as the doors closed.

Larry almost made it to the curb when he was clipped by an oncoming vehicle. Lying in the street, a tangled mess, he was aware of blood pooling beneath his head where it had hit some sharp debris. A good Samaritan gathering with several onlookers bent over him with a handkerchief to press at his wound.

"Call 911," said Larry.

"Do you know the password?" said the woman.

"Nevermind," said another passerby. "Here comes an EMS vehicle."

The attendants, seeing the small group crowding around a fallen pedestrian leapt off the truck.

"Password," asked one of the men at Larry.

"Don't have it," said Larry.

"Sorry, man," said the attendant, "Guess you might have to bleed out. Or..." Larry waited hopefully. "You can visit us on line. WWW...."

And Larry bled out.

Some days later his wife and family were seen to be tearfully gathered around graveside as friends and relatives paid their last respects. The modest little eulogy was quiet and touching.

And as the small group thinned, and Larry's wife and immediate family lingered for a final few moments one of the grave keepers leaned in to Mrs. C. "Do you have your husband's password," he whispered.

"What?" exclaimed Mrs. C.

"The password," said the grave digger.

The grief stricken Mrs. Chumly had no answer.

"Sorry, lady," said the man, as he shouldered his shovel and headed back to the admin building.

It began to rain.

Larry's coffin lay alongside the gaping hole and his wife started rummaging in her bag.

COSMIC RANT

PLUTO

Pluto. Some three and a half billion miles from el sol. (You wouldn't even know it was the sun from out here...; just looks like another of those do nothing stars. And at 26 thousand miles an hour it would take 15 long years to get there...I could probably use the heat) but here I sit. Don't ask.

Incidentally, you might think three and a half billion miles from the center of the solar system (ours) is pretty far out but it's not very much; the entire local business is a dot in the scheme of things, in EVERY direction. (They say it's all flat, you know.) The rest of our home galaxy would take untold thousands of millennia to negotiate from end to end...at light speed - not just a few thousand miles an hour. Perhaps another day, when you and I could chat, I have a few ideas I'd like to impart to you on the subject. Later.

Anyway, good thing I've got a warm jacket. No thanks to speak of from that...sun. Temperatures in this neighborhood have been known, don't ask by whom, to reach nearly four hundred degrees below zero. Chilly. And, worse, did you know almost nothing happens at 400 below? Really. Think of it. Almost *nothing* happens! (Like Washington.) Of course there are colder places; Neptune, for example, with that sea of...whatever it is (don't drink that stuff). Still, when Pluto was the last planet...ah! Back in the day. Anyway, bummer. Everything changes. Maybe someone will get into "climate change" here! (This, however, is difficult in a "climate" in which almost "nothing" happens.)

Meanwhile, you ought to see the view. The stars are very bright. Reminds me of a Breaker Morant poem. (The tent is rigged alright!) Not much light pollution. The landscape is spooky, though. Very. Shiny. Distant. Vacant. It is a little bumpy, but unobstructed...as far as your eye can focus. And very dim, actually. Greenish...but hard to discern tints and shades, really. You know, there is a considerable distinction between shades…and tints! But, it's all kind of dark...so I'm just basically imagining, this - oddly iridescent green. A tad depressing. In fact, more than a tad, I dare say.

Oh, yes. I'm Leominster Melvin. Pleased to meet you.

I realize you are not particularly interested in formalities, so we will dispense with those, and not go on and on like that Willis book "Blackout," which, after more than 500 pages repeating the same song over and over ended with: "to be continued" (in yet another 600 page tome).

What you probably, really, want to know is how in the...world? did I get here. Well, I'm going to tell you, and furthermore I will assure you it will not be such a long and tedious tale as told by Ms. Willis (who must have been compensated by the word. How unconscionable!). This will most definitely not take anything approaching 1000 pages. Ever attempt Atlas Shrugged? Who IS John Galt? But are you comfortable, my friend?

The announcement that changed my life, and not merely a pillow's worth (you might well be aware of the enterprising impresario who sells his pillows to people with the promise of the cushion changing lives…two pillows for the price of one should you be schizophrenic). It had come over the internet, through some kind of adware. I had no recollection of entering the contest of which they spoke, much less winning it, but the announcement people insisted it was me and had got my name, e-mail and home address correct. It indeed appeared that I *had* won and was now the proud recipient of the E-company's new "Friends" application ("app" as it later came to be known and on which I hope to elaborate in another tale) - if I would sign some simple forms and agree to a few basic rules of usage. Why not? So, having dwelt among those who had never won anything, much less anything so new and innovative - and from an E-company - perhaps, I thought, life might actually...improve! Of course, I never had the slightest notion....

Well, the fact was, now that you are perched at the proverbial edge of your seat, as was I, I complied with all instructions forwarded me and appeared at a cold and confusing office building on New York's Sixth Avenue where I was photographed, interrogated, searched, wanded, identified and badged. I then waited and was escorted to a higher floor and a dizzying matrix of doors, was then seated, smiled at, and given an inordinate number of forms and consent slips to peruse and sign.

What would YOU do if you were then simply asked if YOU would like to go to Pluto? Don't laugh. I laughed. I said something I regretted later on and found myself here. I know this resonates with inexplicableness and absurdity. But doesn't so much else in our world?

I could attempt to clarify this adventure, but let's face facts: No one truly cares. No one yearns to join me on Pluto (or probably, anywhere else) and no one believes me. Veracity! Credibility! The believers to whom I harken back: Long John Nebble and his wife Candy, Art Bell, George Norrie and a few others, (abductees on UFOs from Venus) are in the minority. And I'm not sure about George. Long John is long gone.) Anyway, I don't blame any of you…and I, like David Bowman alone on Jupiter, digress. I am, incidentally, distressed to know that the one remaining radio program that would lend an ear to my adventure is currently diluted and not up to the old standards, But standards, like everything else change. And change, is the only fact of life that does not change. Meanwhile, disbelievers abound! Veracity? Credibility? Sorry, my point is approaching.

This is indeed strange. Get closer. Do you recall how so many things vanished in the 21st century? Good films? Then movie houses! Good radio programs? Then radio! Good television programs? Then television! Book stores? Then books! Then libraries! Liberal Arts programs? Then colleges! Remember magazines: Pulps and weeklies? Newspapers? Banks? Post Offices? Mom and Pop shops? All gone! Candy stores? Egg creams, comic books and those boards with tricks and joke: the Joy Buzzer, the Whoopie Cushion, Snapping Gum and the Squirting Ring? The Nail to the Floor Nickel, Sneezing Powder and Hot Pepper Gum? And those two black and white magnetic Tricky Dogs…and the Chinese Finger Trap! All gone!

Remember phone numbers? Remember telephones? Remember actually calling someone, from one of those cozy phone booths…and getting a real human being? Remember conversing with someone other than a cell phone chum? Remember music? Remember real friends? House calls? Doctors? Remember travel? To many of today's people who don't remember, life seems not to have discernibly changed much. But to those who do remember yesterday's REALLY enjoyable flights and movement…travel! Ah! They are aware of the difference between all our evaporated past and the diluted and polluted climate of today. Climate change won't change it. But! Guess what? Good news!

It's all here! Pluto! Had to go somewhere, right? What did Newton say? For every action - a reaction! And who underscored the conservation of matter? Yes! It's dark…it's cold, and it's spooky. But it's ALL here! Yesterday is here! And that kind of warms it up. This is where they put it. Yes, it's depressing if you get your shades and tints mixed up. And almost nothing happens, nothing changes, and it's chilly, but it's not as depressing as you might think. Not at all. But, you know, as I come to think of it, I understand they've even moved Pluto! Is nothing sacred? Well, I've got a warm jacket.

AFTERWORD

At the quantum level, causes of events cannot be accurately determined, in fact, often they cannot even be observed.

Quantum events seem to come into existence on a probability grid...and exist amidst an array of probabilities. So, WE MIGHT ASK, CAN effects, outcomes, on the sub-atomic level have NO CAUSE? And, do particles... perhaps the entire Universe...have their own, self contained, clocks...and THEREFORE follow their own probability schedules?

There are more than a few cosmological theories as to the origins of the Universe but there is one favorite of mine. It states that WHEN it is discovered just how and why the Universe exists...the Universe will vanish...and will be replaced with an exact duplicate.

There is another theory which states this has ALREADY OCCURRED!

THE AUTHOR

GARY ALEXANDER AZERIER IS A FORMER BROADCAST JOURNALIST. HE HAS ALSO TAUGHT COMMUNICATIONS AT FOUR AMERICAN UNIVERSITIES AND DURING A TOUR WITH THE UNITED STATES MARINE CORPS, FOR WHICH HE RECEIVED A COMMENDATION.

GARY RESIDES IN NEW YORK CITY WITH HIS WIFE ROSE ANN.

www.ingramcontent.com/pod-product-compliance
Ingram Content Group UK Ltd.
Pitfield, Milton Keynes, MK11 3LW, UK
UKHW041324190726
13845UKWH00040B/258

9 789363 544062